Commercial and Economic Law in Italy

Commercial and Economic Law in Italy

Second Edition

Gustavo Ghidini
Giuseppe Guizzi
Marcella Panucci
Marco Carlizzi

This book was originally published as a monograph in the International Encyclopaedia of Laws/Commercial and Economic Law.

General Editors: Roger Blanpain & Frank Hendrickx
Volume Editors: Jules Stuyck & Evelyne Terryn

Wolters Kluwer

Published by:
Kluwer Law International B.V.
PO Box 316
2400 AH Alphen aan den Rijn
The Netherlands
E-mail: international-sales@wolterskluwer.com
Website: lrus.wolterskluwer.com

Sold and distributed by:
Wolters Kluwer Legal & Regulatory U.S.
7201 McKinney Circle
Frederick, MD 21704
United States of America
E-mail: customer.service@wolterskluwer.com

ISBN 978-94-035-3425-1

e-Book: ISBN 978-94-035-3430-5
web-PDF: ISBN 978-94-035-3431-2

The Authors

Prof. Gustavo GHIDINI was born in Parma, Italy. In 1968 he taught as associate professor of Intellectual Property law at the Catholic University of Milan, and thereafter in 1970 he became professor at the University of Modena. In 1975 he was appointed full professor at the University of Pavia, Faculty of law. In 1995 he became Professor of Intellectual Property and antitrust law at LUISS University in Rome. In 2003 he became Professor of Intellectual Property at University of Milan. He is now Emeritus at University of Milan, and Senior Professor at LUISS University, Rome.

Prof. Ghidini is also a practicing lawyer specialized in litigation, patent and trademark law, antitrust, unfair competition, copyright and communications law, products liability, and related contractual matters. He is a senior partner at the law office of Ghidini, Girino e Associati (Milan and Rome) since 1992.

He served in several legislative commissions (on IP, antitrust, products liability). He also served as member of the User's Council of the Italian Communication Authority (*Garante della Editoria e della Radiodiffusione*) and of the Advisory Board of the High Commissioner for the enforcement of Counterfeiting. He serves as Member of the Scientific Committee of Queen Mary Journal of Intellectual Property.

His most recent publications include the book Rethinking IP: Balancing Conflicts of Interest in the Constitutional Paradigm, Edward Elgar Publ., Cheltenham, 2018.

The Authors

Prof. Giuseppe GUIZZI was born in Naples, Italy.

He graduated *cum laude* at the Law Faculty of the 'La Sapienza' University of Rome.

He served as Researcher of Commercial Law at the Faculty of Law of the University of Urbino from 1996, and was appointed as Associate Professor of Commercial Law at the Faculty of Economics of the University of Florence in 1998, also teaching Insurance Law between 1998 and 2000 at the same university.

He was appointed as Full Professor in 2000 and has been teaching Commercial Law at the 'Federico II' University of Naples since 2004, where he also taught Insurance Law, Intellectual Property Law and Law of the Sea.

Prof. Guizzi is also a legal practitioner specialized in commercial law, litigation and arbitration, commercial litigation, competition law, and banking and finance law. He is a senior partner at the law firm Ferri, Guizzi, Pagni in Rome.

He is a member of the management team of the *Rivista del diritto commerciale e del diritto generale delle obbligazioni*, of the *RdS-Rivista del diritto societario*, and of the *Corriere Giuridico e dell'Osservatorio di diritto civile e commerciale*. He is the author of numerous essays and monographs on themes such as commercial law, competition law, financial markets law, corporate governance in publicly-held companies and insolvency law. He also authored more than 100 articles published in the main legal journals, on the subject of society, business, debt securities, bankruptcy, competition, banking and financial markets.

He has been cultivating close research relationships with many Universities of Spain since 2007, and particularly with that of Valencia, at which he was a Visiting Professor in 2012.

Marcella PANUCCI graduated in Law with honors from Luiss-Guido Carli University in 1994. She completed her studies at University College London in 1999 under the research program 'The Role of Economics in EC Competition Law'. She obtained a PhD in 'Competition Law' from the University of Perugia in 2004.

Her professional career began in Confindustria in 1995, where she worked as Director of Legislative Affairs until 2011. In 1998, she worked at the European Commission Directorate General for Competition. From November 2011 to July 2012, she was Head of the Technical Secretariat and Economic Advisor to the Minister of Justice. In July 2012, she was appointed Director General of Confindustria, and worked in this role until 2020.

Since November 2020, she has been a Consultant of Cleary Gottlieb Steen & Hamilton LLP and Legal Advisor to the Minister of European Affairs.

Since 2017 she has been Adjunct Professor of Public Law of Economics at Luiss-Guido Carli University, where she was Adjunct Professor of Comparative Corporate Governance from 2014 to 2016, and Deputy Director of the Observatory of Intellectual Property, Competition and Telecommunications.

From 2012 to 2020, she was a member of the Corporate Governance Committee of Borsa Italiana SpA and a member of the Board of Directors of Il Sole 24 Ore. She is currently a member of the Reform for Resiliency Commission, supervisory board member of Human Technopole, board member of Widiba Banca SpA and member of the advisory board of Duferco SpA.

She is the author of publications in the field of economic law.

Marco CARLIZZI was born in Naples, Italy. He graduated at the Law Faculty of the University of Rome 'Tor Vergata' and was then awarded a PhD in Commercial Law from the same University. He was also a Visiting Scholar at the Columbia Law School in New York City.

He collaborates with the University of Naples Federico II and University of Rome LUMSA holding seminars, workshops, tutoring and exams; he is the author of several publications in the field of Commercial Law, Banking Law and Ethical Banks and Finance.

He is currently Partner and Head of Legal Department at RSM Law Firm, as well as founder and present Co-Head of the RSM Legal Group, an institutional group established within the RSM audit and consultancy network.

He has also served as independent director at banks, asset management companies, publicly-owned and listed companies, as well as being statutory auditors for public companies.

He is currently an independent director, and Chairman of the Related Parties Transactions Committee thereof, at a primary Italian and European ethical bank and an independent director at its asset management subsidiary, as well as a statutory auditor at public in-house companies.

The Authors

Table of Contents

List of Abbreviations

ABF	Banking and Financial Arbitrator
ACF	Arbitrator for Financial Disputes
AGEA	Agency for Disbursements in the Agriculture
AGCM	National Competition Authority
AGCOM	National Authority for Telecommunications
ARERA	Italian Regulatory Authority for Electricity, Gas and Water System
CICR	Interministerial Committee of Credit and Savings
CIPE	Interministerial Committee for Economic Planning
CNEL	National Committee on the Economy and Work
COVIP	The Pension Fund Supervision Commission
ENEL	National Corporation of Electrical Energy
ENI	National Corporation of Hydrocarbons
ESCB	European System of Central Banks
IMI	Italian Movables Institute
IPR	Intellectual Property Rights
IRI	Institute for Industrial Reconstruction
ISTAT	Central Statistics Institute
IVASS	Institute for Insurance Companies Supervision
SIM	Italian Securities Investment Firms
VAS	Strategic Environmental Evaluation
VIA	Evaluation of the Environmental Impact

List of Abbreviations

General Introduction

Chapter 1. Geography and Socio-Cultural Composition of the Population

1. Italy is a peninsula bordering, along the Alpine arc, France to the west, Switzerland and Austria to the north, and the former Yugoslavia to the east, and is surrounded in its peninsular extension by the Mediterranean Sea. It is 301,277 square kilometres in area. Within its political boundaries lie the independent territories of the Republic of San Marino and the Vatican City.

2. Italy is a Republic and its capital city is Rome. The country is divided into twenty administrative regions. The language is Italian, although French, German, Slavic and Latin are spoken by minorities in some areas. The majority of the population is Catholic, but there are also minorities practicing other religions.

3. According to the information provided by the Central Statistics Institute (ISTAT), in December 2019 the Italian population was estimated at 60,244,639 inhabitants, showing a decreasing price trend compared to the previous years.

4. In the last century, the Italian population has considerably changed in its numbers, periods and patterns of growth, its social structure, and the movement of the population within the country and abroad.

At the time of Italy's Unification (1861) the total number of inhabitants, within the national borders of that period, was 22,122,000 (corresponding to 26,328,000 in the present borders). This number grew to almost 30 million in 188,133.7 million at the turn of the century, more than 42 million in 193,650.6 million in 1961 and reached 56,324,727 in 1976.

This overall demographic growth, similar to that occurring in the main industrialized European countries, involved important transformations in the age distribution of the population: a progressive decrease in the infantile ages, an increase in the elderly groups as the average life span has extended, and a stabilization in groups of working age. This indicates a continuous ageing of the population.

Along with the demographic dynamics, those phenomena that are related to the geographic distribution of the population, as it has evolved in relation to the recent socioeconomic development of Italy, have been important. We should then keep in mind the important population movements related to the Industrial Revolution, which over the course of a few decades induced massive migrations of the work force toward the regions with a more advanced productive structure. If one considers the volume of migrations absorbed by the cities of the industrial triangle (Turin, Milan and Venice) and by the belt of the Padova Plain, it becomes clear that not only did the disparity between the Northern and Southern regions of the country increase, but also the process of urban growth, strictly connected with immigrations of rural origin, was necessarily accompanied by the consistent phenomena of depopulation of the mountainous and hilly regions.

Finally, an evaluation of the population movement in Italy over the last century cannot ignore emigration abroad, which between 1876 and 1971 involved about 27 million Italians.

Chapter 2. Political System

5. Italy became a unified State in 1861. With the referendum of 2 June 1946, Italy changed its institutional form from monarchy to Republic.

6. The organization of the fundamental bodies of the Republic was established in the Constitution, promulgated on 27 December 1947 and entered into force on 1 January 1948. As the fundamental law of the State, it substituted the Statute ratified by Carlo Alberto in 1848, which had remained in force throughout the Fascist regime.

The first Article of the Constitution defines Italy as 'a democratic republic founded on work' in which sovereignty belongs to the people. The Articles immediately following define the fundamental principles and the rights and duties of the citizens in civil, ethno-social, economic and political contexts.

7. Legislative functions are exercised by the Parliament, which is divided into two branches: the Chamber of Deputies and the Senate of the Republic. They both are elected by universal suffrage for a five-year term.

The President of the Republic is the head of State and is elected for a seven-year term by the Parliament in a bicameral session with the integral participation of representatives of the regions. It is the President's duty to appoint the Prime Minister and (based on proposals by the Prime Minister) the Ministers.

The executive, or administrative, function is exercised by the government, which, representing the parliamentary majority, interprets and carries on the political course.

The jurisdictional function is exercised by the magistrature, whose duty is to administer justice in the name of the Italian people. The magistrature is headed by a superior board (Consiglio Superiore della Magistratura) whose function is to assure the autonomy and independence of the magistrates. The body of supreme guarantee is the Constitutional Court, which judges the correspondence of laws to constitutional principles and the conflicts of authority that occur among the powers of the State, between the State and the regions and between different regions.

8. It should, however, be noted that the concept of tri-partitioning State powers into legislative, executive and jurisdictional (developed by Montesquieu) applied in the so-called capitalist countries has undergone an evolution in which the State itself has been transformed from a simple guardian of legality, extraneous to the lives of individuals, into an active part of the community, a protagonist in social development as well as an intermediary in the resolution of ideological and economic conflicts between social classes. Thus, it is both a 'State of law' as well as a 'Social State'. This evolution has so influenced the traditional concept of separation of powers that there no longer exists a net separation between powers and corresponding functions. In Italy each of the constitutional bodies participates in many functions and is no longer the exclusive depositary of only one of them. The government, traditionally conceived as the administrative body which administratively carries into effect (executive power) the legislative choices of the Parliament (legislative power), is, in the Italian legal system, a participant in the legislative function (decrees and delegated laws).

The Parliament, which institutionally is entrusted with the legislative function and should issue laws of general and abstract content, sometimes also issues specific provisions, (called 'law provisions'), typically acts of the executive power. Furthermore, the legislative and administrative powers are no longer reserved solely and exclusively for the State bodies, but are attributed to other local bodies as well.

9. The Italian Constitution provides for a broad system of local governments, distributed among the regions, provinces and municipalities. In 2001, Italy underwent an important constitutional reform that strengthened the role and powers of regions and local autonomies (Municipalities, Provinces, Metropolitan Cities).

The constitutional reform (Constitutional Law No. 3/2001, voted on 8 November 2001) introduces a new division of legislative powers between the central government and the regions. Prior to the reform, regions were competent only for those matters that the Constitution expressly assigned to them. The new provision enshrined in the Constitution overturns this criterion by expressly listing all subjects reserved to the central government and those governed by concurrent legislative powers of the centre and of the regions. Any other field not expressly reserved to the State falls into the complete competence of regions.

This way, the central government maintains its competences in a number of key areas, such as foreign and defence policy, rights related to citizenship, justice and public securities, protection of the environment, protection of civil and local rights, commercial law, competition law and so forth. Commerce, tourism, local transportations, agriculture, handicrafts and public works are just some of the sectors falling into exclusive regional jurisdiction.

Municipalities have an enhanced administrative role, while regions are in charge with the administration of those subject matters over which they legislate. Moreover, local bodies have autonomous financial resources, partly derived from taxes collected by the State and partly from local taxation and revenue systems. Coordination of public finance falls within concurrent competence.

Chapter 3. Economic System

10. The Italian economic system can be defined as a 'mixed economic system', or an economic system wherein the role of the State is considerable and is closely entwined with private activity. This is not only evident from the weightage of the State budget, but also from the importance of the productive activities under public administration. The privatization process, started in 1992, has changed the main features of the Italian economic system. Nonetheless, the State's presence within the economic system still takes place in different forms: autonomous enterprises (railroads, State monopolies, etc.), and State shareholdings in private corporations. The formula of State shareholdings in private corporations, with the State and private shareholders jointly participating in the administration of enterprises, constitutes a peculiar aspect of public intervention in production in Italy. Productive activities included in the shareholding system are characterized by their considerable global dimensions, as well as by the size of the companies involved and their presence in strategic sectors (energy, defence, etc.).

11. Public intervention has not stifled private economic activity; on the contrary, it has often supported it by creating favourable market conditions, or by bringing private enterprises in difficulty into the State shareholding system, or even by financing in different forms of private economic activities.

As mentioned above, starting from 1992 the Italian economic system has undergone an extensive privatization process. A vast majority of the Italian privatization proceeds have been raised through public offering of shares in the stock market, given the size of assets sold and with the declared purpose of strengthening and widening equity markets. According to the Organization for Economic Cooperation and Development (OECD), public share offerings have accounted for almost 90% of Italian privatization proceeds.

The other main objective of the Italian privatization programme was to alleviate the burden of public debt. Privatizations did contribute to debt reduction rather than to finance deficits. Since 1994, Italy's privatization programme has generated over USD 110 billion: a significant contribution to Italy's improved finances.

12. The Legislative Decree No. 175/2016, which is the consolidated law on public companies, focuses on the incorporation of companies by public administrations, as well as the purchase and the management of shareholdings by these administrations in companies with total or partial public participation, direct or indirect.

Public administrations can hold shares exclusively in joint stock companies and limited liability companies.

Pursuant to the above-mentioned Legislative Decree, public shareholding has two limits:

(1) Strict necessity. Public administrations cannot, directly or indirectly, incorporate companies (as well as purchase and manage shareholdings) aimed at the production of goods and services not strictly necessary to achieve their institutional aims.

(2) Exclusivity of operational areas. Public administrations can, directly or indirectly, incorporate companies (as well as purchase and manage shareholdings) in order to carry out exclusively the following activities:
  (a) production of a service of general interest, including the creation and management of networks and facilities functional to the same services;
  (b) designing and implementation of a public work based on a project agreement between public administrations;
  (c) implementation and management of a public work as well as planning and management of a service of general interest through a partnership contract with an entrepreneur;
  (d) self-production of goods or services that are instrumental to the shareholding public administrations or to the performance of their functions, in compliance with the conditions established by the European directives on public contracts and the relative national transposition legislation;
  (e) procurement services, including ancillary purchasing activities, aimed at supporting non-profit entities and contractors.

13. The Italian economy is strongly integrated at an international level by way of participation of Italy in international institutions (EEC, FAO, WTO, etc.), its world-wide commerce and close ties with foreign businesses through foreign direct investments in Italy and Italian investments abroad and mergers between Italian and foreign companies. Thanks to this integration and to the country's enormous post-war development, Italy can today be defined as an advanced industrial economy. Moreover, while joining the Economic and Monetary Union (EMU), Italy embarked on an ambitious economic reform programme in order to meet the requirements of the convergence criteria of the Maastricht Treaty.

However, a historical weakness of this economic system has not yet been resolved: its territorial dualism, under which a developed North continues to oppose an underdeveloped South. The Italian economy reveals its dualism from another point of view. Under the technological and productive profile, it groups strongly developed sectors, such as manufacturing and mechanical, with sectors that are still backward, such as agriculture. This framework has a significantly detrimental impact on the weight of tax revenues. The persistence of this phenomenon can be explained, in part, by the scarce efficiency of the fiscal system, which, despite a number of attempts of improvement in recent years, is still unsatisfactory. This reveals yet another form of dualism between wide-spread public intervention and the difficulty of finding the necessary (economic) resources to support such intervention; the consequence is heavy public-budget deficit, which negatively affects the economic system.

Notwithstanding recent improvements in regional disparities, employment rates and productivity levels still remain low in the South where a third of the population lives. Policies aimed at reducing the large infrastructural gap of the South, improving the quality of public services and modernizing local administrations can have a significant impact on the output and employment growth and improve the framework conditions under which private agents operate. The process initiated in 1998 and aimed at enhancing local governance systems, has produced different outcomes, such as an increased spending capacity of regions.

Chapter 4. Legal System

14. An outline of the Italian legal system must start with the principle of the 'State of law', which states the supremacy of the law over the State: the State is, therefore, subject to the law and bound to its own laws. As a consequence, the attributions and powers of the apparatus of the State are governed by the law. Thus, they exercise the authority of the State only in the forms and ways allowed under the law. Individuals, in turn, are citizens, and no longer subjects. Their rights and duties are set forth in the fundamental law of the State, the Constitution, and are governed by laws.

15. The legal system can be divided into two large bodies of rules: civil law and public law. According to traditional teaching, civil law is the law that governs relationships among individuals, including the State or other public bodies acting as individuals; public law rules relationships in which the State or another public institution participate with their public authority. In particular, public law governs the conditions, forms and ways of exercising the power of command held by the State and the other public bodies which concur in the exercise of authority (regions and other local autonomies, for example). Public law, therefore, governs: (a) the organization of the State, or rather the formation, the composition and the attributions of its legislative, executive and judicial apparatus, as well as the formation and the attributions of the apparatus of the other public bodies; (b) the authoritative relationships, those based on the exercise of authoritative powers, which the State or other public body establish with individuals or with corporations. The ability to establish authoritative relationships with private individuals is more or less widely recognized. In Italy, as in other European countries, the French model of the so-called State of administrative law has been adopted: the activities of the apparatus of the executive power of the State and those of the public bodies is carried on mainly through authoritative acts (administrative acts), governed by administrative law. The principle of the 'State of law' requires the public administration not to use its authoritative powers except where authorized by the law; in the absence of a provision of law attributing an authoritative power, it remains subject to civil law.

The application of civil law characterizes an extensive sector of public activity: economic activity. Enterprises run by the State or by other public bodies are, with only some exceptions, subject to the same provisions applicable to private enterprises.

16. There are two categories of sources of Italian law: national law, based on the sovereignty of the Italian State, and supernational law, based on the powers of the European Union (EU).

The whole system of the sources of law is made up by:

(1) Constitution and Constitutional Laws.
(2) European Law (Treaties, Community regulations and directives).
(3) Ordinary laws of the State.
(4) Regional laws.
(5) Regulations.

(6) Customs.

This classification of the different sources of the law is associated to a hierarchy of the legal provisions emanated by them: the provisions contained in sources of a higher level must be respected when emanating provisions through sources of lower levels. With regard to local regulations, regional laws and customs the criteria for respecting the provisions of higher levels is combined with those of the context within which each of these sources can operate.

17. Among the different law-making sources are the following:

(a) The Constitution is the fundamental law of the State and the modification of its laws can only be carried out through a special procedure. The procedure for constitutional amendment is set forth in Articles 138 et seq. of the Constitution itself, and it is different from the ordinary law-making procedure (the Italian Constitution has, therefore, the nature of a rigid Constitution and holds a superior position with respect to the other laws of the State for this reason).

The same procedure provided for amendments to the Constitution may be applied to constitutional laws, which can only be adopted to regulate matters reserved – under the Constitution – to constitutional law (*see* Articles 71, 116, 117, 132, 137 of the Constitution). In other numerous cases, the Constitution formulates simple reservations of ordinary law, which means that certain matters cannot be governed by lower sources (*see* for instance Article 42, paragraph 3 of the Constitution).

A provision of law that contrasts with the Constitution or other constitutional laws is called 'unconstitutional'. Not all judges have the power to judge a law unconstitutional. Only a special jurisdictional body, the Constitutional Court, can pass this kind of judgments, with the consequence that laws declared unconstitutional cease to be effective from the day following the publication of the decision (Article 136, paragraph 1 of the Constitution), and are definitively eliminated from the legal system.

(b) The formation of ordinary laws is governed by Article 70 and follows the Constitution; although many laws emanated before the Constitution are still in force. Among these are the Civil Code (hereinafter, also the 'C.C.'), the Penal Code (hereinafter, the 'PC') and the Civil Procedure Code (hereinafter, 'CPC') – however, substantial modifications to the Civil Procedure Code were made with laws 26 November 1990 No. 353, and 21 November 1991 No. 374, and more recently with Law 10 November 2014, No. 162, with the exception of the Criminal Procedure Code that was completely reformed with Decree No. 447 of 22 September 1988 and entered into force on 24 October 1989. The last reform of the Italian Criminal Procedure Code, the so-called 'Orlando's Reform', occurred in 2018. The Civil Code too has undergone a significant reform: the company law reform, which will be the object of Chapter 2.

Government decrees have the same force of ordinary laws. The government can adopt decrees in extraordinary cases of necessity and urgency (though in practice they have become a common instrument of legislation) which lose effectiveness *ex tunc* (i.e. are deemed as retrospectively invalid from the beginning) if, within sixty days, the parliament does not convert them into law (Article 77, paragraph 2 of the Constitution). The government can also issue legislative decrees by parliamentary proxy, on the basis of a law of a delegation which establishes the principles and the directive criteria which the government must conform to and defines the scope of the delegated activity and the period of time within which the proxy must be exercised (Article 76 of the Constitution). During the Covid-19 pandemic (starting from March 2020) the DPCM (Decree of the President of the Council of Ministers) has been one of the most frequently used instrument to deal with the emergency situation.

(c) The EC Treaty and the regulations adopted by the EU Council in the matters set forth by the Treaty are, in the hierarchy of sources, at a higher level than that of the ordinary laws. The inclusion of Italy to the EU has enabled the EU Council to exercise, in the above-mentioned matters, direct powers of law within the individual Member States. Moreover, the European Court of Justice can also exercise direct jurisdictional powers to ensure the application of community law. Therefore, the national judge is bound to disregard the internal laws that conflict with community laws. Regarding the banking system, *see* paragraphs 205-207.

(d) As a result of the constitutional reform of 2001 and of the consequent process of decentralization, regions can exercise legislative powers in a number of matters, without the control of the central government. Regions have exclusive competences in many important areas: agricultural, industrial and retail trade policy; energy production and distribution; mines; tourism; labour policy; water resources; urban planning; regional transport networks; local public services; museums and regional libraries; professional training; local police; social services and other functions.

Other fields are characterized by a shared competence. In those areas the central government sets the general principles and the minimum level of services required at national level. Regional laws enact the framework and implement the principles. In these cases, regional laws cannot be in contrast with the fundamental principles laid down in State laws. All possible conflicts are judged by the Constitutional Court.

(e) Regulations are a source subordinate to the law: they cannot contain provisions contrary to the law and their legitimacy is judged by an ordinary judge (Articles 4 and 3 of the preliminary provisions of the Civil Code); they are issued by the government, as well as by regions and other local autonomies.

(f) At the lowest level in the hierarchy of legislative sources are uses, or customs: an unwritten and non-statutory law-making source. They are constant and uniform practices or given behaviours, carried out with the conviction that such behaviours are legally compulsory. It is held, for example, that banking secrecy is technically a custom: banks refuse to provide the Public Administration (tax collectors in particular) with information regarding their clients under the conviction that they are legally obliged to secrecy, although there is no law providing for this. In fact, it was necessary to issue a law stating that no such obligation existed in order to make it possible for tax collectors to overcome this custom. Although customs hold great importance in Anglo-Saxon countries, in the Italian system the prevalence of the system of statutory law over that of customs is demonstrated by two principles: (1) in matters that are not governed by laws or regulations, customs have full effectiveness (here the absence of State regulation indicates that the State has no interest in governing such matters); (2) in matters governed by laws or regulations, customs are effective only if and when the former refer to them (Article 8 of the preliminary provisions of the Civil Code).

Part I. Commercial Law

Chapter 1. Sources and Principles of Commercial Law

18. Prior to the adoption of the current Civil Code, private law was divided into two different systems of laws contained in separate codes: the Civil Code of 1865 and the Commercial Code of 1865 (and, afterwards, the one of 1882). The Commercial Code not only contained the provisions regarding merchants (currently defined as entrepreneurs) and commercial companies, but also included the law of obligations and contracts, which concurred with those formulated in the Civil Code.

This double system of private law ended in 1942, when a single code of private law replaced the two codes previously in force. The most important aspect of that unification lies in the consequent unification of the two sets of laws on obligations and contracts. The resulting laws were inspired more by the discipline of the Commercial Code than by that of the preceding Civil Code, so much that they are often referred to as a 'commercialization' of private law.

Notwithstanding this formal unification, commercial entrepreneurs are subject to a peculiar discipline set forth not only in Civil Code currently in force but also and, in some cases to a greater extent, in special laws which will be examined in the following chapters.

It is important to mention that the part of the Civil Code that regulates companies has been recently modified. On January 2003, the Italian Government adopted a reform of Company Law (Title V of the Civil Code), through which the previous law, mostly based on the original provisions adopted in 1942, was replaced and updated. This reform process started with the adoption of Legislative Decree No. 58 of 24 February 1998, the Consolidated Law on Financial Intermediation, which laid down a model of corporate governance applicable to listed companies. Therefore, the Company Law reform, which came into force on 1 January 2004, lays down a framework for listed and unlisted companies and fills the regulatory gap created by the Consolidated Law of 1998. Even in 2016, the discipline concerning Italian companies have been further amended by Law No. 116, adopted on 11 August.

Also the Decree Law No. 50/2017, converted into Law No. 96/2017, and the Legislative Decree No. 129/2017 provide for significant amendments to the SMEs legislative regulation. Furthermore, the Legislative Decree No. 14/2019, containing the comprehensive and organic reform of the Consolidated Law on insolvency (the so-called 'Business Crisis and Insolvency Code') encompasses several provisions that directly impact the corporate legal framework. Finally, the COVID-19 outbreak spread out in March 2020 has determined a number of modifications in the commercial provisions of Italian legal system.

Chapter 2. Entrepreneurs

§1. Legal Definition and Discipline of Entrepreneurs

19. According to Article 2082 C.C., entrepreneurs are those who professionally carry on an organized economic activity for the purpose of producing or trading goods or services.

The current Civil Code has substituted the concept of 'merchant', used in the previous Commercial Code, to that of 'entrepreneur' in order to shift the emphasis from the speculative aspect of commercial and industrial activities to their social utility. This development has had an important consequence. At present 'entrepreneurs' are those who run an activity organized with the purpose of 'producing or trading goods or services', whereas 'merchants' were only those who carried out speculative operations as a habitual profession.

The definition of entrepreneur is, therefore, extremely broad: it includes every professional producer or trader irrespective of the purpose of the activity and the circumstance it is profit-making or not. In this regard, it is worth noticing the provision of Article 2093 C.C. that includes among productive activities the production of goods and services run by publicly held companies.

In the Italian system, therefore, the definition of entrepreneur applies to both private and public law, since the pursuit of profit is no longer necessary to acquire the status of an entrepreneur.

The definition of entrepreneur further demonstrates its own broadness as it refers to the nature of the activity: those who engage in an agricultural activity or who exploit the resources of the land (Article 2135 C.C.) are also entrepreneurs, and fall into the same category as those who run an industrial activity, since both produce goods and operate profit-producing activities. Agricultural entrepreneurs, however, are not equivalent in all senses to other (commercial and industrial) entrepreneurs.

In the definition of entrepreneur outlined in Article 2082, agricultural entrepreneurs are distinct from commercial entrepreneurs, who are subject to the most important burdens, which in the previous system were connected to the status of merchant and now constitute the Discipline of Commercial Entrepreneurs.

Article 2086, section 2, C.C. added by the above-mentioned Business Crisis and Insolvency Code, has widened the duties and control measures relating to the management of the enterprise, stating that: *'The entrepreneur, who operates in corporate or collective form, has the duty to set an organizational, administrative and accounting structure that shall be appropriate to the nature and size of the company, also in function of the timely detection of the company crisis and the loss of business continuity, as well as to take action without delay for the adoption and implementation of one of the tools provided for overcoming the crisis and recovering the business continuity.'*

20. In addition to the general provisions on entrepreneurs set out in the Civil Code, which are applicable to all entrepreneurs, specific provisions regarding commercial entrepreneurs provide for the obligation of book-keeping and enrolment in the register of enterprises, as well as subjection to bankruptcy and related proceedings in the event of insolvency.

Commercial activities are as follows:

(1) industrial activities for the purpose of producing goods or services;
(2) intermediary activities in the circulation of goods;
(3) ground, sea and air transport activities;
(4) banking and insurance activities;
(5) activities auxiliary to those listed above.

Those professionally exercising one of the above-mentioned activities are subject to the special provisions established for commercial entrepreneurs, unless they can be qualified as small entrepreneurs.

According to Article 2083 of the C.C., farmers, craftsmen, small merchants and those who engage in professional activities organized mainly with their own work and that of their family members are classified as small entrepreneurs., This kind of entrepreneurs are not subject to the provisions applicable to commercial entrepreneurs. Small entrepreneurs, in fact, even when exercising one of the commercial activities defined by Article 2195 C.C., are not subject (like agricultural entrepreneurs) to bankruptcy or similar proceedings in the event of insolvency (the reformed bankruptcy law provides for some new economic and financial thresholds below which enterprises are not subject to insolvency procedures), and they are not obliged to maintain book-keeping.

Within the general category of entrepreneur, therefore, the Code currently in force distinguishes among commercial entrepreneurs, agricultural entrepreneurs and small entrepreneurs, in order to exempt the latter two groups from the application of the particular provisions pertaining to the first.

§2. Partnerships and Companies

21. The concept of enterprise includes every form of organized economic activities, including both sole proprietorships and partnerships. The Civil Code identifies a set of rules applicable to individual entrepreneurs as well as to companies. To this basic set of rules, provisions regarding companies (Articles 2247 et seq. C.C.) must be added, as well as, for companies whose shares are listed on the stock exchange, the ones contained in Legislative Decree No. 58 of 24 February 1998, the Consolidated Law on Financial Intermediation (hereinafter, also the 'TUF'), and its implementing regulations.

22. The general definition of company is set out in Article 2247 C.C.: 'with the partnership contract, two or more persons confer assets or services for the mutual performance of an economic activity with the purpose of sharing profits.'

23. The different types of companies can be divided into lucrative companies, in case they pursue making of profits, and mutual-type companies, in case they pursue a goal different from the economic one.

From the organizational perspective, companies can be divided into partnerships, where the consideration for partners prevails, who are jointly liable with the company towards creditors, and corporations, where the economic element, represent by the share capital, prevails, and where shareholders are not liable for the obligations of the corporation.

24. Companies are established by means of a multilateral contract with a common purpose, as are associations (Articles 14 et seq. C.C.) and unions of entrepreneurs.

Multilateral contracts allow new parties to join the original ones without the need to execute a new contract.

25. In a partnership contract two or more persons: (a) confer assets or services, (b) for the mutual performance of an economic activity, (c) with the purpose of sharing the profits.

Contributions are assets or services that the parties of the partnership contract are bound to confer; they are no different from any other contractual obligation, except for an additional requirement pertaining to the essence of the partnership contract. Here the parties direct their contributions toward the mutual performance of an economic activity, so that the interests of each party are accomplished through the common activity for which the contributions are planned, and not simply through the obligations of the other parties, unless forbidden by the law. Those who bind themselves in a partnership contract to an obligation of 'doing', or rather, to perform a working activity, contribute 'services'. An obligation of 'giving', on the other hand, involves the contribution of 'assets', intended as any entity which can be economically evaluated (not only money and assets in kind, but also, for example, credits).

In partnership contracts the contributions of assets form a common fund destined to jointly run economic activity. However, the legal status of the assets changes as the assets which are conferred can only be used collectively. Contribution transfers the ownership of the assets from the partner to the partnership; therefore, assets become part of the partnership capital.

26. The mutual performance of an economic activity on the part of two or more persons reveals the link between companies and enterprises. Companies are, in fact, a way to collectively operate 'economic activities'. A company is, therefore, defined by an additional element with respect to an entrepreneur: the economic activity must be performed by two or more persons, but professionalism is not required. Though companies normally originate from the operation of an enterprise, those incorporated for the non-professional (and, therefore, occasional) performance of an economic activity are also admitted.

27. The Civil Code provides for several legal company forms and partnerships. In view of their different characteristics, each type of company is destined to a different function, with a double limitation imposed by the law (Article 2249 C.C.): on the one hand, parties can only choose among the types of companies provided by the law and cannot create new types; on the other hand, if parties decide to set up a commercial activity, they cannot choose the form of the ordinary partnership (‘*società semplice*’), which is only applicable to non-commercial (such as agricultural) activities.

In particular, the Italian corporate system provides for three types of partnerships, the first of which (i.e., the above-mentioned ordinary partnership), as said, is not allowed to engage in commercial activities, while the other two, generally referred to as general partnerships *(‘società in nome collettivo’*) and limited partnerships *(‘società in accomandita semplice’*) can. Apart from some minor differences between their legal regimes, the general principle of the unlimited liability of all partners for the obligations entered into by the partnership still apply to each one of them.

Conversely, the Civile Code as far as companies (‘*società di capitali*’) are concerned, three legal types are regulated, all of which are characterized by the specific feature of limited liability of the participants in the company towards creditors.

Specifically, the Italian legal framework provides for the ‘company limited by shares’, (or ‘joint-stock company’ or simply ‘corporations’) *(‘società per azioni’ or ‘SPAs’)*, the limited liability companies *(‘società a responsabilità limitata’ or ‘SRLs’))* and the limited partnerships with shares *(‘società in accomandita per azioni’)*. The first two types are widespread, the latest one is a legacy from the past, which is substantially no longer seen within the Italian business landscape.

For both SPAs and SRLs, Articles 2446, 2447, 2482*bis* and 2482*ter* set a special management rule, according to which companies shall have a specific ratio between losses and share capital (to be intended as net asset). The Law Decree No. 23/2020 (so-called *‘Decreto Liquidità’*), converted into Law No. 40/2020, adopted in order to face the emergency due to the outbreak of COVID-19 pandemic, derogates to such rule, providing that, until 31 December 2020:- in case of losses such as to reduce the share capital by more than one-third or below the legal minimum, Spa and SRL are exempted from the obligation to recapitalize or convert the company; and in case of loss or reduction of the capital below the legal minimum for Spa and SRL the cause for dissolution specifically provided for by Article 2484, para. 1 no. 4, of the Civil Code for Spa and SRL shall not apply.

28. Società per azioni – SPAs (public limited company). The discipline of SPAs, whose general rules laid down in Articles 2325 et seq. C.C., is differently graduated according to the degree of the company’s openness to the public. Open SPAs, those that make use of the risk capital market and, hence, have dispersed ownership, are characterized by a higher degree of mandatory rules, which are necessary in order to protect third parties’ interests, while ‘closed’ or ‘private’ SPAs, with a concentrated ownership, are characterized by more flexible rules.

In both cases, procedures for incorporation have been simplified with the reform of 2003 and the scope for fund-raising broadened (different types of shares and shareholder loans are allowed, limits on bond issues are eased). In 2014, the so-called ‘Competitivity Decree’ (Decree No. 91/2014), reduced the minimum share capital amount required for the incorporation of a public limited company, from EUR 120,000.00 to EUR 50,000.00. However, in any case the company must be incorporated by way of public deed, the ‘deed of incorporation’, *(‘atto costitutivo’*) before a public notary. The specific rules governing the company, which must be compliant to the Italian corporate law, are contained in another document, attached to the deed of incorporation, called company by-laws (*'statuto sociale'*), which, on the contrary to the deed of incorporation, is subject to possible further amendments during the lifetime of the company, as deemed necessary or advisable by the corporate bodies, upon resolution by the shareholders' meeting passed with an increased majority compared to the ordinary resolutions by this meeting.

29. The company's capital is composed by contributions, which are the assets transferred by the shareholders to the company at the time of its incorporation or later during the company's lifetime, that are actually attributed to the nominal share capital. In SPAs. The contributions, according to Article 2342 C.C. must be done in cash, unless the by-laws allow for contributions in kind. Contributions in cash shall be paid to a bank account immediately upon incorporation by shareholders in a percentage equal to at least 25% of the value of the shares subscribed. The directors will request the shareholders to pay the residual portion of the share capital when they repute it necessary or useful. This provision does not apply in the cases of a SPA with a sole shareholder (*'s.p.a. unipersonale'*), in which the contribution must be entirely paid at the time of its formation. In SPAs, contributions of assets in kind and/or credit are also permitted; however, in this case, pursuant to Article 2343 C.C., the shareholder must submit the sworn report by an expert designated by the court in whose district the company is based, containing the description of the assets or credits conferred, the attestation that their value is at least equal to that attributed to them for the purpose of determining the share capital and any share premium, with indication of the criteria of evaluation being followed. Such report must be attached to the deed of incorporation.

On the contrary, the performance of works or services cannot be conferred in exchange for the underwriting of shares in SPAs, while these types of contributions are permitted for the other more flexible corporate type, the SRLs, as explained in detail under paragraph 38 below.

As a general principle, each shareholder is allotted a number of shares proportional to the value of contribution made. The by-laws can provide for a different, disproportional allocation of shares, and, in such case, the surplus will be allocated to available capital, in the same way as if it were a share premium.

Conversely, under Article 2346, section 5, C.C., in no case whatsoever the aggregated value of contributions can be lower than the total amount of the company share capital. This represents a key principle of the Italian corporate legal framework with regard to capital formation rules, which strictly forbids the overvaluation of contributions, while allowing the opposite, as described above.

This prohibition is aimed at protecting other shareholders, investors, corporate creditors, and any third-parties in general, from the misrepresentation of the real amount of corporate assets available for the pursue of business objectives that would arise from any artificial inflation of a company's capital base, as a consequence, in turn, of a valuation of contributions that exceeds their real value.

Particularly, the former would be prejudiced if the portion of the share of capital attributed to the shareholder/s who made a contribution in kind were higher than the actual value of the goods or receivables conferred.

The same applies to investors, corporate creditors and third parties, who would rely on a fictitious, higher company's capacity if the value represented by the contributions in kind proved to be overestimated.

Another key provision related to the above fundamental rule on capital formation is the special regime applicable, as per Article 2356 C.C., to shares corresponding to portions of capital whose price/contribution has not yet been paid *('azioni non liberate')*. Said article provides that, if such shares are transferred, the seller is jointly and severally liable, together with the buyer, for the payment still due for three years from the date on which the transfer is recorded in the company's registry of shareholders.

30. With specific regards to the transfer of shares, the law allows for the deed of incorporation and/or the by-laws to establish limits to the free circulation of stocks. The most common ones are, respectively, the so-called lock-up *('divieto di circolazione')*, approval *('gradimento')* and pre-emption *('prelazione')* clauses, which can be inserted, either in the by-laws or in shareholders' agreements, or in both. The first of such provisions causes the shares not be transferrable for a maximum period of five years, the second makes the transfer of shares conditional to the approval of a certain corporate body (usually the board of directors) or of other shareholders. It must be noted, however, that, pursuant to Article 2355*bis* C.C., an approval clause that does not indicate any criteria or reasons upon which the transfer is conditional *('clausola di mero gradimento')* is not effective if it does not provides, in case the approval is denied, either the obligation by the company or the other shareholders to acquire the shares in question, or the right to withdraw for the shareholder willing to sell the shares. Finally, the pre-emption clause obliges the shareholders to offer the shares they intend to sell to the other shareholders, prior to be lawfully entitled to finalize the transaction with their selected counterparty.

31. The characteristic feature of shares is that, as opposed to bonds, which are securities that grant the bearer only the rights arising from the status of creditor, they do not represent a right of credit towards the company, but a percentage of the company capital. Hence, shares do not only attribute their owner a right to profits and a right to a *pro quota* portion of the residual corporate assets in case of liquidation, as well as to the option rights and the right to withdraw as main economic rights, but an entire series of so-called 'administrative rights', such as the right to intervene, in certain cases even call, and vote in meetings, to appeal against invalid resolutions of the shareholders' meeting (limited to those who did not intervene in that meeting or did not agree with the passed resolution), to consult the register of shareholders and the register of the general meetings and resolutions.

Article 2348 C.C. states that, as a general principle, shares must be of equal value and confer equal rights to their holders applies.

Nonetheless, the deed of incorporation or subsequent modifications of the by-laws can provide differently, allowing the issuing of special categories of shares with different rights. One of these categories is preference shares: their holders are given a higher quota in the division of the profits and the distribution of the assets resulting from liquidation (Articles 2350 and 2351). Preference shares can be shares with limited voting rights: within the aggregate limit of one half of the company share capital, the by-laws can in fact provide for shares: (i) without voting rights, (ii) with voting rights limited to particular topics, or (iii) subject to particular conditions that must not be purely discretionary, and (iv) multiple-vote shares, which can grant a maximum of three votes each.

The by-laws may also provide that, in relation to the quantity of shares held by the same person, the right to vote is limited to a maximum amount or be staggered.

Other categories, are shares in favour of workers, as per Article 2349 C.C., and profit shares *('azioni di godimento')*, as per Article 2353 C.C. The latter concur only in the distribution of profits remaining after the payment of shares which were not reimbursed with a dividend equal to the legal interest rate, and in the distribution of the company's capital remaining after reimbursement of the other shares at their nominal value in the event of liquidation.

In general, it is noteworthy that, pursuant to Article 2376 C.C., if different categories of shares are issued, general shareholders' meeting resolutions that prejudice the rights of any one of them must be approved also by special meeting of shareholders of the interested category.

32. Governance systems in SPAs can be structured in three alternative forms: the traditional (Italian) model, with a board of directors ('*consiglio di amministrazione*') or a sole director ('*amministratore unico*'), save as provided for listed companies pursuant to Article 14*ter* TUF), and a board of statutory auditors ('*collegio sindacale*'); the two-tier (German) model, with an executive board and a supervisory council; and the one-tier (Anglo-Saxon) model with a board of directors that appoints its own internal audit committee. However, the traditional model remains the most common form of governance structure deployed by Italian joint-stock corporations.

In SPAs, as anticipated, the corporate capital is divided into shares and the main corporate bodies are the shareholders' meeting, the management body, composed as above, and the board of statutory auditors.

33. The shareholders' meeting is the collegial deliberative body, composed by every physical or legal person holding shares that grant them the right to vote, which basically means the owners of ordinary shares, with the exception of particular types of shares that does not confer voting rights to the owners), and their right to vote is certified in accordance with the terms and the procedures set forth by the statutory provisions in force from time to time. The shareholders' meeting can be ordinary or extraordinary, depending on the specific matter to be resolved.

As per Article 2364 C.C., the ordinary shareholders' meeting is held, usually at least once a year, to resolve about several fundamental matters, which pertain exclusively to this body to deliberate. Focusing on the traditional system, these matters are:

(a) The appointment of the management body (the board of directors or the sole director).
(b) The appointment of the board of statutory auditors and of its Chairman, as well as, if required, the person/s or the company entrusted with the legal auditing of accounts *('revisione legale dei conti')*.

(c) The determination of directors' and statutory auditors' remuneration, if not already set forth by the by-laws.
(d) The approval of the Financial Statements of the company.
(e) The initiation of claims and/or actions against directors and statutory auditors.
(f) Any other matters assigned by law to its competence and also on any authorizations required by the by-laws to the fulfilment of acts of directors.

Instead, Article 2365 C.C. the extraordinary shareholders' meeting is competent to resolve upon amendments to the by-laws, the appointment, termination, replacement, and powers of the liquidator/s, and any other matter attributed to it by law.

In any case, the shareholders' meeting is called by the company's management body, also upon request by shareholders who represents a percentage of at least the one-twentieth of the outstanding capital in the open companies and at least the one-tenth of the capital in the private companies, or the lower percentage set forth by the by-laws, provided that the shareholders indicate the items on the agenda of the requested meeting.

Both the shareholders' meeting constitution and the passing-resolution *quora* vary between the ordinary and the extraordinary meeting.

In particular, the Civil Code provides that:

(i) the ordinary meeting is duly convened with the presence of at least one half of the outstanding share capital, excluded the shares that do not attribute voting rights to the owners, and resolves with the favourable vote of the absolute majority of the share capital represented, unless the by-laws sets forth an increased majority, while;
(ii) the extraordinary meeting resolves in any case with the favourable vote of more than half of the outstanding share capital, unless the by-laws sets forth a further increased majority; in case of open companies (as said, the ones that make use of the risk capital market) the extraordinary meeting is duly convened when at least half of the share capital is represented, unless the by-laws sets forth an increased threshold, and resolves with the positive vote of two-third of the represented capital.

Specific, lower quota are established for the meetings in second call, which occur when a prior meeting did not reach the required constitution quorum. Second-call ordinary meetings must resolve on the same items set forth in the agenda of the first meeting, whichever the percentage of the share capital represented at the meeting, while the extraordinary meetings are duly convened with the presence of more than one-third of the share capital and resolves with the favourable vote of at least two-third of the represented capital.

With specific reference to open companies, ordinary meetings in single or second call are duly convened whichever the percentage of the share capital represented, and resolve with the absolute majority of the votes represented; extraordinary meetings require the presence of at least one-fifth of the share capital (unless the by-laws sets forth an increased majority) and the positive vote of at least two-third of the represented capital. However, some crucial matters require by law in any case a higher percentage of positive votes to be resolved, with the aim of preventing majority shareholders from passing modifications that substantially alter the key features of the company without the consent at least of a certain part of minority shareholders.

As a consequence, Article 2369, section 5 C.C. private companies must resolve in any case, including second-call meetings, matters such as amendments to the business purpose, the transformation of the company, the transfer of the registered headquarters of the company abroad, the extension of the duration of the company, the advance liquidation of the company, the revocation of the liquidation, the issuance of shares with a limited or staggered voting rights with the positive vote of more than one-third of the share capital.

34. According to Article 2380*bis* C.C., the administrative body is solely entitled to, and responsible for, the management of the company, it is elected, as said, by the shareholders' meeting and also non-shareholders may be appointed as directors. When more than one director is appointed, the must act and resolve as a collegiate body, specifically as a board of directors. The directors appoint among them the Chairperson, if he/she has not previously appointed by the shareholders' meeting.

For the purposes of the daily management of the company, the by-laws may entrust the board of directors with the power to delegate most of its functions to an executive committee (*'comitato esecutivo'*). To the same aim, the directors also appoint among themselves one or more Managing Director/s, entrusted with a wide range of management powers, and sometimes even with the legal representation of the company towards third parties. Other directors may also be granted specific, less wide, powers, which must be recorded as well in the Register of Companies, for the purposes of giving third parties proper information about the scope of the powers of each director. The members of the board of director whom have not been given specific powers are referred to as non-executive directors (*'amministratori non esecutivi'*), which are subjected to a particular status, and related duties, as a consequence of their lack of powers to act individually on behalf of the company.

Directors are appointed by an ordinary shareholders' meeting for a maximum period of three financial years, unless a shorter period is provided for in the by-laws, and their office terminates at the date of the shareholders' meeting convened for the approval of the financial statement of their third year of mandate; however, they may be reappointed for the same maximum period.

Directors' office ceases on: (i) expiry of their mandate, and, in this case, the directors remain in charge of the ordinary management activity until the newly appointed director accepts the appointment; (ii) resignation; and (iii) revocation by the ordinary shareholders' meeting for whatever reason, although if no justified reason exists the director/s may claim damages against the company.

Meetings of the board of directors must be attended personally by no less than the majority of the directors and resolutions are passed with the positive vote of the majority of them. On the contrary to shareholders' meeting, in which proxies are to a certain extent allowed, no vote by proxy is permitted nor may a director appoint a substitute to attend or vote in his place, even temporarily.

Powers, as well duties, of the board of directors have been widened and strengthened by the latest corporate law reform, and their duties and responsibilities have been made clearer and differentiated between the executive and non-executive members of the board. In line with the provisions of the Consolidated Text on Financial Intermediation (Testo Unico della Finanza – TUF), the enforcement of directors' liability has been made easier to exercise by qualified minority shareholders.

As anticipated above, the general task of the board of directors under Article 2380*bis* C.C. is to implement the company's corporate purpose and to ensure that it is achieved in compliance with the law, by managing and supervising the conduct of the company's business. Therefore, both the ordinary and the extraordinary management of the company are exclusively entrusted to the directors, which are entitled to carry out any transaction aimed either at implementing, also indirectly, the corporate purpose of the company, within the limits set out by the law, by the company's by-laws, or by the other corporate bodies, especially the shareholders' meeting, which, for instance, may provide for a delegation and/or a limitation of powers to certain directors.

35. The Civil Code provides that all directors must fulfil the duties imposed upon them by the law and by the company's by-laws.

As a consequence, directors are bound by a certain number of general duties, the main of which are:

(i) the duty of care and/or diligence, and to respect the principles of sound administration, as per Article 2392, section 1, C.C.: all directors must diligently fulfil the duties imposed upon them by law and by the by-laws with the standard of diligence required by the nature of their office, taking into account the specific competence of the director; they are jointly liable towards the company upon failure to comply with the above-mentioned duties;

(ii) the duty of loyalty, indirectly inferable from Article 2392, section 1, C.C., and also specified as the duty to carry out business in the best interests of the company, disregarding any other interfering interest, including those of other group or affiliated companies, notwithstanding possible 'management and coordination' or group policies affecting the free decision-making process of the company; according to the same duty of loyalty, directors must not misappropriate the assets of the company or use these for purposes other than the company's corporate objects;

(iii) the duty of disclosure, as per Article 2391, sections 1–4, C.C.: new rules on conflicts of interests require board members to notify the other directors and the board of statutory auditors of any personal interests they may have, directly or indirectly, on their or on third parties' behalf, in any operation under consideration. The Civil Code has also provided for a specific discipline of conflicts of interests connected to related-parties transactions in listed companies, empowering National Securities and Exchange Commission (CONSOB) to adopt enacting rules (per Article 2391-bis C.C.). The Authority has adopted a regulation in early 2010. In particular, each director must disclose any personal interest in company matters or transactions, by indicating the nature of the interest in the transaction, and its terms, conditions and origins. Where the relevant director is the Managing Director, he must also abstain from carrying out the specific transaction individually and submit it to the board of directors. In the above circumstances, the resolution by the board of directors is legitimate only if it clearly indicates the reasons and the opportunity for the company to approve the relevant transaction. Resolutions adopted by the board of directors which do not observe the above requirements, or which have been approved with the vote of the interested director, if harmful to the company, may be challenged by the directors or by the board of statutory auditors, although remaining in any case effective towards bona fide third parties (i.e. third parties acting in good faith);

(iv) the duty of confidentiality, as per Article 2391, section 5 C.C.: directors are also obliged not to use for their own benefit, or for the benefit of a third party, data, information or opportunities of the business of which they becomes aware during their office;

(v) the duty of ensuring adequacy (as regards executive directors), as per Article 2381, section 5, C.C.: every delegated body/director ensure that the organizational, administrative and accounting structure is adequate to the nature and size of the company and report to the board of directors and the board of statutory auditors, with the frequency established by the by-laws, and in any case at least every six months, on the general management trend and its foreseeable evolution, as well as on the most significant transactions, due to their size or characteristics, carried out by the company and its subsidiaries;

(vi) the duty to act on an informed basis, as per Article 2381, section 6, C.C. For this purpose, each director is entitled (and indeed should regard himself as required) to ask the Managing Director or any other executive director/body constantly to provide the board of directors with all information related to the management of the company;

(vii) the duty of early detection of the crisis, as per the revised Article 2086, section 2. C.C.: the directors must establish an organizational, administrative and accounting structure which is adequate to the nature and size of the company, also in function of the timely detection of the crisis of the company and the loss of business continuity, as well as to take immediate action for the adoption and implementation of the instruments provided for by the law for overcoming the crisis and recovering business continuity;

(viii) the duty not to compete with the company, as per Article 2390 C.C.: unless previously authorized by the shareholders' meeting or by the company's by-laws, a director cannot be a partner with unlimited liability in a competitor of the company, nor a director or a general manager of a competitor of the company, nor carry out any activity which may be considered as being in competition with the company's activity for his own interest or on behalf of a third party. In cases of breach of such duty, the director may be revoked by the board of directors and shall be liable for any damages suffered by the company.

36. The last compulsory corporate body in SPAs is the board of statutory auditors, which is appointed by the shareholders' meeting for a period of three years, and is entrusted with the duties of supervision on the compliance with law and by-laws provisions, compliance with the rules of appropriate management and internal controls, and, in particular, on the adequacy and reliability of the organizational, administrative and accounting structure adopted by the company and on its functioning. The board of auditors is jointly liable with the board of directors.

The board of statutory auditors is comprised of three or five permanent members and two auxiliary members, at least one of whom must be enrolled in the Register of Auditors held by the Ministry of Justice. It cannot be revoked except for just cause, and the dismissal resolution must be approved by means of a decree of the local court, having heard the board concerned.

In SPAs, the company's by-laws may also entrust the legal auditing of accounts to the board of statutory auditors if the company is not required to prepare consolidated financial statements. Otherwise, in case the drafting of such consolidated statements is mandatory, the appointment of a Registered Auditor or an Audit Firm registered within the Roll of Auditors at the Minister of Justice is also compulsory. When the board of statutory auditors is in charge also of the legal audit of the company accounts, all its members must be registered auditors.

Among other tasks, the board of statutory auditors must prepare a report on the financial statements that includes an assessment on accounting, the reliability of the financial statements and the results of the audit performed during the financial year. This report must then be submitted to the annual general meeting.

As the board of statutory auditors, as explained above, performs a key function in supervising the compliance with law and the by-laws by the other corporate bodies, as well as the corporate functioning as a whole, it has the power to conduct inspection and control activities, obtain information, reports and documents from the board of directors on any corporate matters and transactions, even with regard to controlled companies.

Moreover, under Article 2406 C.C., the board of statutory auditors is also responsible for convening the shareholders' meeting should the directors fail to do so, and to execute the required publications; pursuant to section 2 of the same article, in case it is deemed necessary, it can also convene the shareholders' meeting upon its own initiative, when it discovers critical facts of significant gravity and there is an urgent need to deal with them.

Finally, as the corporate supervisory body, the board of statutory auditors is the designated recipient of official complaints from any of the shareholders, under Article 2408 C.C., and is obliged to take into account such complaints in drafting its report to the shareholders' meeting. If the complaint is lodged by at least one-twentieth of shareholders in private companies, or by at least one-fiftieth of them in open companies (i.e., those that makes use of risk capital market), the board of statutory auditors is mandated to investigate without undue delay in respect of said complaints and present its conclusions and possible proposals thereto to the shareholders' meeting and, where deemed necessary under the above-mentioned Article 2406, section 2, C.C, call a shareholders' meeting.

37. Società a responsabilità limitata – SRLs (limited company). As anticipated above, the new discipline of SRLs (Articles 2462 et seq.) is characterized by a very high degree of flexibility, which led the SRL to be the most used legal type for the incorporation of Italian companies; in 2017, according to the data collected by

ISTAT ('Archivio Statistico delle Imprese Attive' by ISTAT), the SRLs in Italy amounted to about 880,000, while the SPAs were about 30,000. Many aspects that were formerly regulated by the law are now subject to self-regulation, by means of the by-laws. There are still some mandatory provisions in force, in order to maintain the 'fiduciary relationship' among shareholders, which is pivotal to this corporate form. Therefore, enhanced shareholder rights to request information, to bring lawsuits, and to withdraw in cases of dissent are provided.

In addition to the standard SRL type, with a minimum share capital equal to EUR 10,000.00, the Italian legislator recently provided for the possibility to incorporate a SRL in a simplified form, with a minimum share capital from EUR 1,00 to EUR 10,000.00, pursuant to Article 2463*bis* C.C.

38. With reference to SRLs, Article 2464 C.C. states that the value of the contributions cannot be overall lower than the global amount of the share capital.

All the elements of the assets susceptible to economic evaluation can be conferred, including the performance of work or services, which is one of the key features that made the SRLs legal regime different from the SPAs one, as above described.

Unless otherwise established in the deed of incorporation, the contribution must be made in cash.

At the signing of the deed of incorporation, at least 25% of the contributions in cash and the entire premium or, in the case of a unilateral deed, their entire amount must be paid to a bank. For the contributions of goods in kind and credits, the provisions of Articles 2254 and 2255 apply. The shares corresponding to these contributions must be fully paid up at the time of subscription.

Another key difference in capital formation rules is that, for SRLs, is that the contribution can also take place through the provision of an insurance policy or a bank guarantee through which the obligations assumed by the shareholder making a contribution relating to the provision of work or services in favour of society are guaranteed for the entire value assigned to them. In this case, if the deed of incorporation provides for it, the policy or the guarantee can be replaced by the shareholder with the payment of the corresponding amount in money to the company as a deposit.

If, at a certain point, only one shareholder is left, the payments still due must be made within ninety days.

According to Article 2465 C.C., anyone who confers assets in kind or credits must submit the sworn report of a statutory auditor or a statutory auditing company registered in the appropriate register. The report, which must contain a description of the assets or credits conferred, an indication of the valuation criteria adopted and the attestation that their value is at least equal to that attributed to them for the purpose of determining the share capital and any premium, must be attached to the deed of incorporation.

If the shareholder does not carry out the transfer within the prescribed period, the administrators warn the defaulting shareholder to carry it out within thirty days.

If this term has elapsed in vain, the directors can sell the share of the defaulting shareholder to the other shareholders in proportion to their participation. The sale is carried out at the risk and peril of the same for the value resulting from the last approved financial statements. In the absence of offers for the purchase, if the by-laws allow it, the share is sold at auction.

If the sale cannot take place due to lack of buyers, the directors exclude the shareholder, withholding the sums collected. The capital must be reduced accordingly.

The defaulting shareholder cannot participate in the decisions of the shareholders.

39. Governance rules in SRLs are not heavily regulated and the law allow company's by-laws a wide degree of latitude.

SRLs can be managed by a sole director or a board of directors or, alternatively, by more directors acting jointly or severally but not forming a board of directors.

The directors of an SRL can be other than quota holders, if expressly provided in the by-laws. In any case, this meaning also if a board of directors is not established, the functions that cannot be delegated and must be resolved upon collectively by the directors' regard: (i) the increase of the capital, pursuant Article 2481 C.C.; (ii) the drafting of the annual financial statements, and (iii) the drafting of merger and demerger plans.

The by-laws may contain further provision for: (i) requirements, powers and duties of the directors, to which some rules set forth for SPAs' directors may apply, if compatible; and (ii) that resolutions be adopted in writing (i.e. without a physical meeting).

A sole auditor (external or internal), or, on a residual basis, an internal supervisory board, can be provided for by the by-laws, but is not mandatory, unless certain thresholds (e.g., regarding number of employees, turnover or assets) are exceeded. As anticipated above, the Decree Law No. 32/2019 *('Decreto Sblocca-Cantieri'),* converted with amendments into Law No. 55/2019, has recently lowered such parameters, providing for EUR 4 million as total assets, EUR 4 million as annual turnover, and an annual average of twenty employees as the thresholds that, if at least one of them is exceeded for two consecutive years, oblige the company to appoint a supervisory body in the form of a sole auditor, unless the by-laws sets forth otherwise.

If mandatory, or so provided for in the by-laws, supervision can be exercised by an internal auditor, or if expressly so allowed in the by-laws by a board of statutory auditors) or, alternatively, by an external auditor, in accordance with the provisions of the by-laws.

40. As anticipated above, the Decree Law No. 50/2017, converted into Law No. 96/2017, has provided for significant amendments to the SMEs framework.

The just mentioned Decree Law realized a disruptive change in the regulation of SMEs established in the form of SRLs. Such decree, in fact, extends to SRLs that fall into the definition of SMEs, due to their limited size, the vast range of exceptions previously envisaged only with reference to innovative start-ups and innovative SMEs, resulting in a very different regime, compared to the traditional one, as applicable to SRLs so far.

It is a far-reaching amendment, which involves most of the Italian SRLs, considering that the definition of SMEs generally referred to is that contained in the Recommendation of the European Commission 2003/361/EC, which qualifies as an

SME an enterprise that has less than 250 employees, an annual turnover not exceeding EUR 50 million, and/or an annual balance-sheet total not exceeding EUR 43 million.

Initially, with the D.L. 18 October 2012, n. 179 *('Decreto Crescita bis')*, converted into Law No. 221, the legislator has introduced some exceptions to the corporate code regulations in relation to innovative start-ups set up in the form of SRL, in order to promote all those entrepreneurial activities characterized by an innovative footprint. The main amendments regard the possibility for those companies of:

- providing in the deed of incorporation categories of shares provided with different rights (in derogation from Article 2468, sections 2 and 3, C.C.);
- creating categories of shares that do not attribute voting rights or that attribute voting rights to the shareholder in an extent that is not proportional to the participation held by him, or voting rights limited to particular topics or subject to the occurrence of particular conditions that are not merely discretionary (in derogation from Article 2479, section 5, C.C.);
- carry out transactions on their shareholdings if the operation is carried out in implementation of incentive plans that provide for the assignment of shareholdings to employees, collaborators or members of the administrative body, service providers and professional services (in derogation from Article 2474 C.C.);
- provide that equity interests in innovative start-ups established in the form of SRL may be the subject of an offer to the public of financial products, including through the raising of capital, within the limits provided for by special laws (in derogation from Article 2468 section 1, C.C.).

Through the Decree Law 33 24 January 2015, the so-called *'Investment Compact Decree 2015'*, this exemption were extended also to innovative SMEs and UCIs that invest in shares or units of the aforementioned companies.

Subsequently, the scope of application of the above-mentioned exceptions was further extended with Law No. 232/2016 ('Stability Law 2017') to all SMEs, even to those lacking the requirement of innovativeness of their corporate purpose.

Article 57 of the Decree Law No. 50/2017 (the so-called 'Corrective Decree') has extended, by amending the previous Article 26 of the Growth Decree 2.0, the exceptions provided for therein in Article 2468, sections 1, 2, 3, Article 2474 and Article 2479, section 5 C.C. to SRLs that, at the same time, qualify as SMEs, which are the majority of them.

41. To a certain extent, in light of this legislative innovation, it is possible to consider such SRLs/SMEs as equivalent as SPAs, only in a smaller size.

In fact, they both share the exemption to the prohibition of offering the participation of shareholders or quota holders to the public, set forth by Article 2468, section 1, C.C., which no longer operates with specific regard to SMEs in form of SRLs, as well as it is the case for SPAs.

As a paramount consequence of such innovation, SMEs/SRLs are now able to attract investment by the offering of securities to the public through online platforms, thus accessing alternative and more effective forms of financing, namely the equity crowdfunding, rather than being limited obsolete means, such as business angels and venture capital.

Likewise, notwithstanding the provisions of Article 2468, paragraph 2 of the Italian Civil Code, SMEs-SRL may derogate from the principle of proportionality between the corporate rights and the participation owned by the shareholders.

Furthermore, the new legislative paradigm expressly allows SMEs/SRLs to create categories of quotas provided with different rights, also derogating from the principles enshrined in sections 2 and 3 of Article 2468 C.C. and Article 2479, section 5, C.C.

This is a disruptive change, especially taking into account that the possibility for creating participations that embed particular rights, pursuant to Article 2468 C.C., as resulting from the latest reform of Italian corporate law, does not endorse the creation of special categories of quotas.

All SMEs/SRLs, therefore, can now create different categories of depersonalized participations that regulate the relationship between the investment risk and the management power of the company in the way that best suits the needs of the various parties involved. With the significant difference, compared to SPAs, that SRLs are not required to comply with the limit set forth by Article 2351 C.C., which states that shares without voting rights or limited voting rights may not, overall, exceed the half of the company share capital.

Finally, with regard to the prohibition for SRLs to purchase or accept their own participations as collateral, Article 57 of the Decree Law No. 50/2017 permits SMEs/SRLs to carry out transactions on their shareholdings, if the transaction is performed in implementation of incentive plans that provide for the allocation of shareholdings to employees, collaborators, or members of the administrative body, work or service providers (the so-called 'work-for-equity' plans).

42. Cooperatives (società cooperative). The reform has stressed the pursuit of the social function and mutualistic purpose connected to this legal form and introduced the class of cooperatives 'with prevalent mutual nature', with 51% of their activity being of a genuinely mutualistic nature. The reform has also strengthened the capacity of this company form to access capital markets.

43. The company law reform has introduced brand new rules concerning groups of enterprises, with the purpose of enhancing the responsibility of the controlling entity and protect the interests of shareholders and creditors of controlled companies. Shareholders and creditors can sue the controlling entity for damages resulting from violations committed by its managers.

Moreover, the clear identification of both controlling and controlled companies must now be officially registered and the consolidated group balance sheet reported in addition to the ordinary reports.

Finally, the possibility to withdraw from the controlled company is provided in favour of shareholders in cases of change of control, when the company is not listed on the stock market.

Article 2497, as modified by the Code of Crisis, states that the companies or legal entities that, in the exercise of management and coordination towards other companies, act in their entrepreneurial interest or in the interest of third parties, infringing the principle of proper management of the companies, shall be deemed directly liable towards shareholders and creditors of the companies, in case of prejudice to the value of shareholding or damage to the capital assets. No liability shall be found in case of the overall positive result of the management and coordination, or in case the damages have been eliminated.

44. As already pointed out, Article 2247 specifies that parties must collectively carry on an economic activity, 'with the purpose of sharing the profits'. The purpose of adhesion to the partnership contract and of the consequent contribution is making profit. In order to be considered a company, an enterprise must be conducted for profit, and that profit must be divided among partners. The purpose of profit differentiates companies from enterprises and associations.

The pursuit of profit is not necessary for an economic activity to be classified as a business activity, and therefore the definition of 'company' does not comprise every form of collectively operated enterprise, but only that of the collective enterprise run for the purpose of profit.

In the context of collective enterprises, companies are those collective enterprises whose purpose is profit. When a business activity is operated for the accomplishment of idealistic or other non-economic goals (e.g., cultural, political or charitable), collective enterprises will still be present, in view of the fact that costs must still be covered by income, though these collective enterprises cannot be qualified as companies, but only as associations. These are in fact collective enterprises operated for non-profit, idealistic purposes and established and legally organized in the form of an association, the regulation of which is contained in the first book of the Civil Code (Articles 14 et seq.). By adopting the 'Third Sector Code' in 2017 with Legislative Decree No. 117, the Italian legislator has recently reorganized the set of rules applicable to not-for-profit entities while providing stricter limits and additional advantages.

In particular, the not-for-profit entities shall:

- enrol in a special Register;
- be subject to the obligation of book-keeping;
- appoint an audit body.

45. Within the contest of the social enterprise, a new model has been recently adopted: the benefit corporation. It has been introduced for the first time in US, where the regulation is mainly inspired to the 'Model Benefit Corporation Act' (so-called 'Model Act'), drafted by the non-profit organization B-lab, supported by the American Sustainable Business Council.

The main elements of a benefit corporation are:

- the general public benefit, to be inserted in the memorandum;

- the new conduct standards to be imposed to directors, according to which the duty of care and the duty of loyalty shall now refer even to the public benefit of stakeholders;
- specific transparency obligations, which include the publication of an annual report and the compliance with third party standard.

From 2007, the benefit corporations can obtain a special certification, issued by B-lab, which qualifies, upon strict evaluation, as 'Certified B Corporation' or 'B Corp'.

In Italy, the benefit corporation has been introduced by Law No. 208/2015; in this case, the general public benefit to be fulfilled is not considered a third social purpose, other than the profit or non-profit one, but it deemed as a complementary purpose, that can be pursued by profit or non-profit entities.

§3. Innovative Start-Up

46. In late 2012, Italy introduced a comprehensive legislative framework with Law Decree No. 179 of 18 October 2012, the so-called 'Italian Startup Act' (ISA) aimed at fostering the creation and growth of its startup ecosystem.

Innovative startups are defined as limited companies (including cooperatives), that meet the following requirements:

- they are newly established or have been incorporated for less than five years;
- they have their legal seat in Italy, or in another EU/EEA Member State provided that they have a production facility or a branch in Italy;
- they have an annual turnover lower than EUR 5,000,000.00;
- they do not distribute their profits, and have not done so in the past;
- their social purpose concerns, predominantly or exclusively, the development, production and commercialization of innovative products or services with a clear technological component;
- they are not the result of a company merger or split-up, or of a business or branch transfer;
- finally, they meet at least one of the three following innovation-related indicators: (a) research and development expenditure corresponds to at least 15% of the higher value between turnover and annual costs (as per the last statement of accounts); (b) the total workforce includes at least one-third of PhDs, PhD students or researchers, or at least two-third of the team hold a master's degree; (c) the company is the owner or licensee of a registered patent (or it has filed an application for an industrial property right) or it owns an original registered software.

An innovative startup that meets the above-mentioned requirements may, on request, be qualified as an innovative startup with a social purpose if, in addition, it operates in any of the sectors identified by national legislation on social enterprises.

Chapter 3. Economic Institutions

§1. Public Economic Institutions

I. The Bank of Italy, the CONSOB, the ISVAP, the AGCM, the AGCOM the AEEG and the COVIP

47. The capital market is divided into three areas: the credit system, the insurance system and the movables market. Corresponding to the credit system are the supervisory bodies of the Interministerial Committee of Credit and Savings (CICR), the Minister of Economy and the Bank of Italy. The insurance system is supervised by the Institute for Insurance Companies Supervision (IVASS), which, with effect from January 2013, took over from ISVAP, as provided by Law No. 135/2012. The movables market is supervised by the Treasury and CONSOB.

The supervision of the credit and insurance fields is mainly concerned with the legitimacy and merits of operations, and at times a true directive power. The supervision of the movables market is mainly concerned with the clarity, completeness and truthfulness of the information offered to investors.

The transformations which have taken place in the general model of economic development in Italy have brought about modifications in the financial structure of the country, particularly in relation to banking, corporate and insurance fields, thus making public intervention necessary.

The functions of the supervisory bodies have broadened, although they have been put into practice without a uniform law, responsible for, in some cases, a lack of provisions and, in others, an overlapping of provisions (such as cases of supervision by both the Bank of Italy and CONSOB or IVASS and CONSOB).

Transience of the limits between credit, insurance and finance activities sometimes causes conflicts among supervisory bodies which are often resolved by the legislature through mechanisms of reciprocal information.

Measures were adopted in 2005 (with Law No. 262) in response to financial scandals, in order to strengthen controls over financial markets and dispose a different balance of powers within the authorities. The powers of CONSOB have been enhanced in order to ensure more effective controls on financial markets and prevent any risk of fraud. The new rules also strengthened the role of CICR in supervisioning the system.

48. Banking supervision, born to safeguard interests emerging from the operation of the credit activity, is now arranged according to the provisions on the organizational structures of the credit system and to the regulation of the quantitative data on money allocated in the banking sector.

Such interventions, very thorough in practice, are made legally possible by the vast discretion allowed by the current system of banking legislation. It provides a complex pyramidal system of credit that has developed through the passing of numerous laws (*see* the Legislative Decree No. 385 of 1 September, 1993, the Consolidated Text on Banks).

The tip of the pyramidal system is today represented by the CICR, the Minister of Economy and by the Bank of Italy.

CICR is entrusted with the high supervision in matters concerning the guardianship of savings and credit functions, as well as monetary matters.

The committee is a collegiate body, chaired by the Minister of Economy (former Minister of Treasury), that has the administrative role of direction and coordination (Legislative Decree No. 691 of 17 July 1947; Article 1 of Legislative Decree No. 626 of 30 March 1968).

The functions of supervision of the credit institutions are exercised in complete autonomy by the Bank of Italy, the National Central Bank, founded in 1893 as a joint-stock company and subsequently honoured as an institute of public law.

The Bank of Italy is part of the European System of Central Banks (ESCB) and of the Eurosystem. It pursues general interests in the monetary and financial sector, such as maintaining price stability and ensuring the stability and efficiency of the financial system. The Bank of Italy concurs to the decisions on monetary policy in the Eurozone and enacts them at the national level; is responsible for the production of the Euro currency, according to the quota fixed at European level; promotes the regular functioning of the payment system.

The Bank of Italy is in charge of the effective governance of credit, carried on through the duties of direction, vigilance and control over the entire credit field. For that purpose, the Bank of Italy has the power to execute the directives and decisions of CICR, in addition to the functions of consultation and resolution, namely authorization (i.e., the authorization to issue securities and real properties to be sold through credit institutions or to be quoted on the stock exchange), approval (i.e., approval of capital increases and issuances of bonds by the credit institutions), appointment (e.g., the appointment of directors and provisional commissioners of credit firms in mergers), admissions (e.g., the enrolment of credit firms in the proper register), orders (e.g., orders to convene meetings in the credit firms) and consent (i.e., the approval to take over management of revenue offices).

In order to perform its supervisory activities, the Bank of Italy has policing powers, aimed at ensuring that the banks carry out their activities in compliance with proper requirements, and powers of direction for safeguarding, through the coordination of the different activities, the functional capacity of the banking firms, as well as powers of inspection (periodic or occasional).

Finally, the Bank of Italy carries out banking activities like direct discount of assets, exchange deferrals with credit firms, advances on public debt securities of the State and so on that confer on it the role of the bank of banks.

49. The Commissione Nazionale per le Società e la Borsa (CONSOB) is the public authority responsible for regulating and supervising the Italian financial markets, also referred to, in the EU legislation and regulation, as the Italian 'National Competent Authority' (NCA).

CONSOB is a legal entity of public law, introduced into the Italian system with Law No. 216 of 7 June 1974, and is made up of a president and four members appointed by a presidential decree. CONSOB is a member of the Committee of European Securities Regulators (CESR).

The mission of CONSOB is to guarantee investors' protection and the efficiency, transparency and development of the financial market.

For this purpose, on one side, CONSOB regulates the provision of investment services; minimum capital requirements for companies who manage regulated stock markets; the drafting and publication of prospectuses and documents to be published when securities are offered to the public or admitted to trading; procedures for the execution of public offerings; disclosure requirements for listed companies. On the other side, CONSOB authorizes the exercise of regulated markets; the publication of prospectuses; the exercise of the activity of centralized management of financial instruments; the enrolment in public registers.

In order to guarantee investors' protection CONSOB exercises supervision over listed companies.

The law provides for a complete and accurate disclosure of information on ownership of issuers (persons holding, directly or indirectly, more than 3% of share capital, or 5% if the issuer is a small and medium-size enterprise), relevant shareholdings, potential relevant shareholdings, board members. CONSOB has to ensure that the information provided to the public is timely, complete and accurate.

As mentioned above, CONSOB has also to ensure the accuracy of facts and information represented in the prospectuses for the offerings of securities to the public. Law No. 77 of 23 March 1983 expanded the supervisory powers of CONSOB, providing that any offer to the public of stocks, convertible and non-convertible bonds, or of any other movable value must be communicated to the Commission, with an indication of the quantities and characteristics of the securities offered. The publication of an informative prospectus is compulsory. From the prospectus the organization, the economic and financial situation and the evolution of the company carrying out the operation must be inferred.

The same law has extended pre-existing controls over listed companies to the companies controlling them and controlled by them. Any solicitation to the public (made for example through public adverts, door to door sales, circulars or by means of mass communication) must be authorized by CONSOB.

CONSOB has the power to request listed companies to draw up a consolidated balance sheet even for homogeneous areas; it can order that facts and information concerning the company be made public. It can even demand periodic communication of information and the transmission of acts and documents for integration with those indicated on the balance sheet, in the exhibit of balance sheets and in the quarterly reports; it can establish the ways and times in which public offers must be made available to the public. It has the power to contest the resolutions of the general meeting of listed companies suspected of violating their obligation to communicate the shareholdings considered quantitatively important. Finally, CONSOB can contest consolidated balance sheets.

CONSOB's supervision is extended to intermediaries (Italian Securities Investment Firms - SIM, non-EU investment firms, trusts, EU investment firms). From 1 January 2009 the financial salesmen register is no longer held by CONSOB but by the Authority for the Single Register of Financial Salesmen.

Law No. 157 of 17 May 1991, which introduced provisions aimed at preventing and repressing insider trading and distortions of the prices of movables values. These provisions have been widely amended by Law No. 62 of 18 April 2005, which enacted the EU Directive on Market Abuse. From 16 April 2014 all the provisions concerning Market Abuse were expunged from the Italian Consolidated Law on Financial Provisions and the rule were included in the Market Abuse Regulation (EU) 596/2014, which entered into force on 3 July 2016. CONSOB remains the competent authority for the purposes of this Regulation (with the exception of the competences of the judicial authorities).

CONSOB is also empowered to apply administrative pecuniary sanctions in specific cases of infringements that are regulated by the TUF. Its President has also the exclusive power to press criminal charges.

Finally, as far as the supervision of the stock market is concerned, until 1974 it was the responsibility of the Treasury Department to supervise directly the stock exchange. It fixed the stock exchange calendar, determined of the types of exchange contracts admitted and the modalities of formation of the stock exchange list, and checked that the exchanges functioned correctly. In 1974, these tasks were transferred to CONSOB that was entrusted with the direct supervision of the stock market.

In 1998, securities markets were privatized, therefore, the organization and management of regulated markets of financial instruments was assigned to the Italian Stock Exchange (Borsa Italiana), a public limited company, whose shareholders are the main Italian banks, intermediaries and issuers. Its main objective is to guarantee the development and maximization of liquidity, transparency, competitiveness and efficiency of markets. In 2007, Borsa Italiana merged with the London Stock Exchange. In the aftermath of this merger, the Alternative Investment Market (AIM) Italia has been established. It is a marketplace dedicated to dynamic and competitive SMEs, looking for capital to finance growth thanks to a balanced regulatory approach, designed for the needs of ambitious companies. AIM offers a quotation path calibrated on the structure of small and medium-sized enterprises, based on the central figure of a consultant – the Nomad – that assist the Company during the admission phase and for the entire stay on the market.

50. Insurance companies collect, through premiums paid by the insured, vast financial means, and thus conduct a function of collection similar to that performed by banks. For this reason, insurance firms are also subject to supervision by a special public body instituted with Law No. 576 of 1982: the ISVAP.

In conformity with the course fixed by Interministerial Committee for Economic Planning (CIPE) (*see* the following paragraph) and the directives of the Minister for Economic Development, ISVAP is responsible for the control and supervision of the entire field of insurers.

51. Law No. 287 of 10 October 1990 (the Competition Act) instituted the National Competition Authority ('Autorità Garante per la Concorrenza e il Mercato' or AGCM), a collegial body composed of a President and four members, appointed by the presidents of the Chamber of Deputies and the Senate.

Substantive rules on competition are derived from the European framework. Therefore, the Italian Competition Act prohibits anticompetitive agreements and abuses of a dominant position. The Act sets out rules for the evaluation/ authorization of mergers.

The Authority is also empowered to apply community law to practices which affect trade between Member States and take place in the national geographic market or within a substantial part of it. The Authority's powers are similar to those granted to the European Commission.

The Authority can act on its own initiative or on a complaint. In these cases the Authority opens an investigation, which is notified to the parties involved. The Authority has broad powers of assessment: it can require undertakings, associations of undertakings or persons involved to provide information and exhibit documents which might be useful for the investigation; order inspections aimed at checking companies' documents and take copies of them, also through the cooperation of other State bodies; order expert opinions and economic and statistical analyses as well as the consultation of experts with respect to any aspect relevant to the object of the investigation. Fines are provided for those who do not comply with such requests.

If upon conclusion of the investigation – after hearings and debate with all interested parties – the Authority finds out an infraction, it fixes a term within which the undertakings or association of undertakings concerned must bring the infringement to an end; it can also impose fines, taking into account the gravity and duration of the infringement, accept commitments, or give exemptions or a negative clearance. An additional power, similar to that recognized to the European Commission, is the possibility to conduct general inquiries in the economic sectors in which the development of trade, the performance of prices, or other circumstances, lead to the presumption that competition is impeded, restricted or altered.

The Competition Act does not provide for criminal sanctions or penalties against individuals. Therefore, the main sanction for the enforcement of competition rules is of a pecuniary nature. General rules concerning fines have been amended by Law No. 57 of 2001, which abolished the minimum percentage provided for by Article 15 of Law No. 287 of 1990 and set forth for the application of fines up to 10% of the total annual turnover of the undertaking and are similar to those provided for in Reg. 1/2003. In 2014, the National Competition Authority adopted new Guidelines on fines aimed at defining a specific calculation method; for instance, having regard to price fixing, market sharing and limitation of production, a minimum percentage equal to 15% of the value of sales has been established. Furthermore, the Authority has designed the possibility of further increasing sanctions in certain cases. In 2014, the Authority has been recognized even with powers relates to the consumers' protection.

Like other Member States and the European Commission, the Italian Law also provides for a leniency programme, according to which the Authority can grant immunity from fines to an undertaking disclosing its participation in an alleged cartel, if that undertaking is the first to submit information and evidence, following which the Authority can carry out an investigation and find out an infringement. Other undertakings disclosing their participation to a cartel may be eligible to benefit from a reduction of fines.

Since 2004, the Authority has the competence to apply the Law No. 215 of 20 July 2004 to conflicts of interests in the public sector.

Finally, in 2018, the National Competition Authority has been recognized with the power of evaluate the enterprises according to a special rating of lawfulness.

52. The Communications Authority (AGCOM) has been instituted by Law No. 249 of 31 July 1997. The two main tasks assigned to the Authority are to ensure adequate conditions for fair competition in the telecom market and protect fundamental rights of all citizens.

The Authority is made up of a plurality of bodies: the president, the Commission for Infrastructures and Networks, the Commission for Services and Products, the Council. Each Commission is a collegiate body and is composed by the president and four commissioners. The Council is composed by the president and all commissioners.

The president of the Authority is appointed by the President of the Republic with a decree, upon proposal of the president of the Council of Ministers in agreement with the Ministry of Communications. The nomination shall be submitted to the competent Parliamentary Commissions for approval. The Senate of the Republic and the Chamber of Deputies elect four commissioners, each of whom is subsequently appointed with a decree of the President of the Republic.

The Authority's mission is to protect both operators and consumers and follow the implementation of the liberalization process in the telecommunication market through regulation and supervision activities. Consumers' concerns in the field of communication are addressed by carrying out a control on quality and distribution of services and products, including advertising. The Authority has also to foster and safeguard political, social and economic pluralism in broadcasting. A system of alternative dispute resolution has been set up by the Authority in respect of disputes arising between operators and among users and operators. The task of defending copyright of audiovisual and software products has been recently added to the main ones by establishing a Unit against piracy within the Authority.

53. The Italian Regulatory Authority for Electricity, Gas and Water System (ARERA), formerly National Authority for Electricity and Gas (AEEG), has been created by Law No. 481 of 14 November 1995. The Authority was set up on 4 December 1996 and has become fully operational since 23 April 1997 with the main task of regulating and controlling the electricity and gas sectors. The Authority has to ensure uniform availability and distribution of services related to electricity and gas throughout the country and establish a transparent and reliable tariff system based on pre-defined criteria, thus safeguarding and promoting the interests of users and consumers. Legislative Decree No. 102/2014, implanting the Energy Efficiency Directive 2012/27/EU, conferred the Authority further specific functions concerning district heating and cooling; moreover, Law No. 205 of 2017 attributed to ARERA responsibilities and sanctioning powers related to control over the waste cycle.

Its regulatory powers include the setting of tariffs and the definition of service quality standards and the conditions governing access and interconnections to the networks for services where technical, legal or other constraints would interfere with normal competitive market conditions and with the ability of the market to protect the interests of users and consumers.

The board of the Authority is composed by a president and four members appointed by the Council of Ministers upon proposal of the Minister for Economic

Development. Nominations are submitted to the competent Parliamentary Committees for scrutiny, and the appointment is ratified by the Parliament with an absolute majority vote. To ensure their independence, commissioners are forbidden to maintain professional relations with any company operating in the regulated sectors during their term of their office and the subsequent two years.

54. Legislative Decree No. 124 of 21 April 1993 established a Commission (Commissione di vigilanza sui fondi pensione – COVIP) in charge of the supervising the functioning of pension funds. The Commission is a collegial body made up of the president and four commissioners. Law No. 144 of 17 May 1999 has strengthened the Commission's resources and powers and granted considerable autonomy in determining its organizational structure and functioning.

Notwithstanding the lack of formal independency – the Commission has links with the Ministry of Labour and the Ministry of the Treasury – COVIP enjoys a high degree of autonomy and has several important tasks, for example, to authorize the setting up of new pension funds; keep a register of authorized pension funds; supervise the administration and the technical and financial operations, asset management, and accounting of pension funds; make recommendations on funds' accounting obligations.

II. The CIPE, the CICR and the CCIAA

55. Interministerial committees, boards made up of more than one minister, constitute articulations of the government, with a view to the realization of a coordinated system for accomplishing goals of public interest.

In most cases, they are presided by the Prime Minister or by a minister delegated by him/her. The committees of greater importance operate directly in external relationships and carry out functions of coordination and direction.

56. The CIPE is composed of the Prime Minister and sixteen other ministers involved in the economic affairs. It represents the centre in all governmental activities in economic matters. It is responsible for the preparation of the national economic policy (Law No. 48 of 27 February 1967, modified by Law No. 17, 24 June 2013), and it annually approves the forecast and planning reports of the economic policy, as well as the relative planning of the sector and the guidelines of the Italian budget and annual budget of the State. Furthermore, it approves pluriannual programmes containing the objectives of the extraordinary interventions of the State. It establishes the general regulations in the field of scientific and technological research development and coordinates the use of the relative financial resources. It indicates the planning goals for housing, approves plans for the division among the regions of the national funds assigned to housing, draws up the national energy policy, and so on.

57. The CICR has been instituted in 1947; it is composed by the Minister of Economic and Finance, Minister of Production Activities, Minister for Agricultural and Forestry Policy and the Minister of Environment. It is the authority supervising on credit sector and on protection of savings and it resolves upon proposal by Bank of Italy, implementing the necessary measures to realize the economic objectives set by the government.

58. Still within the sphere of public economic institutions, are the Chambers of Commerce, public entities in which all members of professional categories (industry, commerce, handicraft and agriculture) must take part.

Chambers of Commerce have a public law status. Legislative Decree No. 580/1993 reorganized the rules concerning Chambers of Commerce, industries, crafts and agriculture underlining their independence. Chambers of Commerce are subject to the supervision of the Minister of Economic Development. They can issue regulations concerning their internal organization and administrative functions which are subject to ministerial approval. Their function is to coordinate and take care of the interests of the categories they represent and promote and advise political action to that end, keep the Register of enterprises, form market statements, assess and note local habits and customs that are of concern in economic matters and publish the lists of protests.

Legislative Decree No. 580 has been reformed by the Legislative Decree No. 23 of 25 February 2010. The Decree strengthened the Chambers' actions in the fields of internationalization and promotion of Italian enterprises abroad; simplification; promotion of innovation and technology transfer. The Chambers can also exercise some functions upon delegation by the State or by regions.

More recently, with Legislative Decree No. 219/2016, a broad reform concerning functions and financing mechanism of Chamber of Commerce was adopted; in such context, the reform established a new territorial distribution criteria by providing for a minimum dimensional threshold equal to 75,000 enterprises enrolled in each register. Decree No. 219 also amended and re-defined tasks and functions allocated to chambers of commerce (i.e., legal publicity functions, consumers' protection, support to companies' competitiveness, organizational support and assistance to SMEs).

§2. Private Institutions Involved in the Resolution of Disputes

I. Arbitration and Mediation

59. As already pointed out, the Italian judicial system is based on two levels of jurisdiction plus one of legitimacy (before the Supreme Court of Cassation), but in commercial matters, it is becoming more common to assign the settlement of disputes to private arbitrators instead of turning to ordinary courts. The reason for this recourse to forms of 'private justice' can be found, on the one hand, in the greater speed with which a decision may be reached and, on the other, in the specialization of private arbitrators in complex matters and in the confidentiality of the procedure.

This way, parties stipulate a special agreement, called arbitration, or they insert a clause (arbitration clause) in a pre-existing agreement whereby they undertake to remit to trusted third parties (arbitrators) disputes which may arise from the same agreement.

There can be one or more arbitrators but always in an odd number, and the arbitration clause must already include their nominations or indicate the criteria for their nomination.

The proceeding, which has the same structure as ordinary court proceedings, is disciplined by the eighth title of the Civil Procedure Code. It is nevertheless a private judgment whose judicial structure is not adequate to attribute to the decision (called arbitrament) the full effectiveness of a sentence issued by an ordinary judge. The parties, or one of the parties, may choose, within the peremptory term of one year, to make the award effective like an ordinary sentence (Article 825 of the Code of Civil Procedure). To do so, the award must be deposited in the Registry office of the Magistrate's Court by the concerned party and the judge, upon verifying the formal regularity of the award, will confer effectiveness to the award by order.

60. 'Ritual' arbitrations (those complying with the provisions of the Civil Procedure Code) are different from 'non-ritual' arbitrations (not governed by the Civil Procedure Code), which have their substance in the employment of arbitrators to settle a dispute not as 'private judges' but in the exercise of the same contractual powers with which the parties themselves could resolve it. In such cases, the arbitration does not have the structural characteristics of a court proceeding, but is comparable to a settlement agreement, and thus the conclusive act of non-ritual arbitrations has nothing in common with a sentence, and, for this reason, cannot acquire the same effectiveness.

61. Finally, Article 1349 of the Civil Code provides for 'arbitrage' which, quite unlike arbitration, consists of the parties' deferring to a third party the determination of the considerations inferred in the contract or the integration of another element of the contract at the conclusion of the contract. In this case the arbitrator does not settle a dispute, which has not yet arisen, but settles a generic conflict of interests at the time of the contract's execution.

62. In 2010 a new form of alternative dispute resolution mechanism – mediation – was expressly regulated by law. Mediation is the professional activity carried out by an independent third party and aimed at assisting two or more parties in finding an agreement for the settlement of a dispute.

Legislative Decree No. 28 of 4 March 2010 has provided for three different types of mediation: compulsory, delegated by the judge, voluntary. Mediation is compulsory for disputes concerning civil liability for damages caused by car or boat accidents; co-property; real rights; rental agreements; inheritance; divisions; medical liability; libel through press articles; bank, insurance and financial contracts. In these cases parties cannot go to court if they have not made a trial to mediate.

A compulsory mediation has been deeply renovated in 2013 with Law No. 98, by which the Italian legislator restored such procedure in the legal system as a consequence of the declaration of constitutional illegitimacy adopted by the Constitutional Court in 2012. With Law No. 96/2017 the legislator has confirmed compulsory mediation for claims related to the matters listed in Article 5, paragraph 1 *bis* of the Legislative Decree 28/2010 (e.g.; real property rights, lease contracts, lease of business, inheritance).

Unlike arbitrators, the mediator only helps the parties in finding a mutually convenient agreement, but is not entitled to take a decision. If the parties reach an agreement, its enforceability is submitted to the judge-type approval. The decree provides that a mediation proceeding cannot last more than four months.

Along with the mediation, the Law Decree 132/2014 has introduced a new form of alternative dispute resolution mechanism: the assisted negotiation. It is an agreement between the parties, aimed at an amicable settlement of the controversy.

A previous negotiation is compulsory for claims related to traffic accidents and in case of claims for compensation whose amount does not exceed EUR 50,000.00.

63. Law No. 262/2005 has imposed banks and financial intermediaries to participate to alternative dispute resolution mechanisms. Therefore the Banking and Financial Arbitrator (ABF) has been created. This entity is organized and managed by the Bank of Italy and is entitled to treat disputes arising from banking contracts. The same Law has also introduced a Chamber for Conciliation and Arbitration within the CONSOB in order to decide disputes arising between non-professional investors and banks or other financial intermediaries regarding the breach of transparency and information requirements provided by contracts regarding investment services or collective saving management. From 9 January 2017, has been instituted the Arbitrator for financial disputes (ACF) provided for by the Legislative Decree No. 130 of 2015 in implementation of the EU directive 2013/11/EU. The ACF, established by CONSOB with Resolution No. 19602 of 4 May 2016, is a tool for resolving disputes between 'retail' investors and intermediaries for the breach of the obligations of diligence, correctness, information and transparency that intermediaries must respect when providing investment services or the collective management service of savings.

II. Advertisement Jury

64. In the Italian system, there is a 'court' having jurisdiction specifically over the field of advertising.

Since the 1950s there was a need for behavioural rules in this field, in order to discipline advertising, given its importance and utility in the economy, as a public information service.

Thus, 'Codes of Ethics' were created by individual organizations of various fields of the time. In 1966 a unified code was established and became the first Italian code of self-discipline in advertising. A second edition followed in 1971 and a further revision brought the present code, enacted on 1 March 1975.

The Self-Regulatory Code of Commercial Advertising
(*'Il Codice di Autodisciplina della Comunicazione Commerciale'* 68th edition, effective from 9 February 2021) is based on a premise, illustrating its objects and sphere of application, a paragraph containing the definitions of the concepts of 'advertisement', 'product' and 'advert' and forty-six articles divided in two parts. The first part of the code sets forth the general rules applicable to each type of advertisement, while the second gives the specific requirements for advertisements in each individual product area and for certain forms of sales.

65. The enforcement of the rules set out in the code is entrusted to two bodies of self-discipline, the Jury and the Assessment Committee, to which the second and last part of the code is dedicated. The Jury is a legal body with an essentially jurisdictional function. The Assessment Committee is a technical body with duties of a tutorial type, and has the power to file actions before the Jury in the interest of consumers.

The Committee is a collegiate body composed of jurists, advertising operators, and representatives of firms and consumers (Article 30). The Code attributes the Committee various important functions: the fundamental function of filing, of its own initiative, actions before the Jury; that of requiring the advertiser to prove the truthfulness of the affirmations made in the advertisement; that of inviting the advertiser, as a preventative measure, to modify advertisements that appear not to comply with the rules of the Code; and that of preliminarily expressing its own opinion on the conformity of the not yet distributed advertisement to the rules created for consumer protection.

In concrete cases and upon the solicitation of the Assessment Committee or other concerned parties, the Jury, as a body of self-discipline with jurisdictional power, has the authority to enforce the rules of this self-disciplinary system. The decisions of the collegiate judge are enforceable, and since there is no higher court before which to appeal the Jury's sentences, they are definitive.

The trial scheme is reduced to the essentials, but guarantees the fundamental principles of plaintiff-defendant intervention (Article 36), indication of the charges, which guarantees that the parties are informed of the object of dispute (Article 37), debate (Article 38), defence and the possibility to file an opposition (Article 39) and the communication of the decision (Article 40).

In addition to issuing decisions in the cases brought before it, the Jury is the only body authorized to impose the prescribed sanctions. The most important is the order to desist from the reproved behaviour (Article 39). At its discretion, the Jury may additionally order the publication of the sentence (Article 40). Finally the code provides a response to cases in which the condemned party does not comply with the sentence and continues in the acts it should have desisted from: in such cases the sanction consists of publicizing the non-compliance through the most appropriate means of communication (Article 42).

III. Specialized Courts on Intellectual Property Rights and Company Law

66. On July 2002, the Parliament approved a law that empowered the government to create twelve specialized Intellectual Property Rights (IPR) courts and to adopt rules to reorganize several aspects of intellectual and industrial property law. The government was given broad powers also with the aim of achieving full harmonization with EU and international laws concerning intellectual property rights.

Article 16 of Law No. 273/2002 provided for measures to reorganize judicial proceedings concerning the enforcement of intellectual property rights. The government (Legislative Decree No. 168/2003, entered into force on 12 July 2003) has, therefore, created a plurality of specialized sections having jurisdiction on national and community trademarks, patents, utility models and designs, copyright and unfair competition.

Specialized sections have been created within the districts of Bari, Bologna, Catania, Florence, Genova, Milan, Naples, Palermo, Rome, Turin, Trieste and Venice.

67. The competence of the specialized sections has been recently extended by Decree No. 1/2012 in order to include company law, civil cases arising from public procurement contracts above the EU economic thresholds and antitrust infringements. During the parliamentary proceeding for the conversion of the Decree into Law, the network of specialized sections has been geographically extended. Specialized sections therefore have been created in twenty courts belonging to almost all Italian regions. However, in the European perspective shall be also pointed out that in 2016 the Unified Patent Court Agreement has been ratified and executed in Italy with Law No. 214, which is closely connected with subsequent laws concerning the implementation of the unitary patent.

Chapter 4. Register of Enterprises and Book-Keeping

68. Register of Enterprises and book-keeping are regulated by 2214 et seq. of the Civil Code.

The authors of the Civil Code had conceived a system of legal disclosure for commercial entrepreneurs, to be put into effect by means of a special Register of enterprises (Article 2188 of the Civil Code). Although the provision dated 1942, it was only enacted in 1993, with Law No. 580 and the Register made operational in 1995.

The registration at the Register of Enterprises is mandatory for the entrepreneurs who exercise the following activities:

(1) an industrial activity aimed at the production of goods or services;
(2) an intermediary activity in the circulation of goods;
(3) a transport activity by land, water or air;
(4) banking or insurance activity;
(5) other activities ancillary of the previous ones.

Within thirty days from the start of the business the entrepreneur who carries out a commercial activity must request the registration at the Register of Enterprises in whose district he establishes the office, indicating:

(1) the surname and the name, the name of the father, the citizenship;
(2) the company name;
(3) the purpose of the business;
(4) the company headquarters;
(5) the surname and the name of the agents and attorneys.

The entrepreneur must also request the registration of the modifications relating to the aforementioned elements and the termination of the company within thirty days from that in which the modifications or termination occur.

Subject to the obligation of registration at the Register of Enterprises are general partnerships, limited partnerships, joint stock companies, limited partnership with shares, limited liability companies and cooperative companies, even if they do not exercise a commercial activity. Also subject to the obligation of registration at the Register of Enterprises are public bodies whose sole or principal purpose is a business. Instead, small business owners are not required to register at the Register of Enterprises.

69. Commercial entrepreneurs are required to keep continuous documentation of their activities by performing appropriate book-keeping. This documentation functions as an instrument of control on the activity of commercial entrepreneurs, in the interest of those who enter into business negotiations with them and acquire credits in their regard. The interests protected are those of individual creditors who can base the proof of their claims toward the entrepreneur on the book-keeping. Furthermore, they are the interests of the group of creditors in the event of insolvency of the commercial entrepreneur. In cases of insolvency, by examining the book-keeping, it is possible to ascertain the consistency of the bankrupt's capital, to reconstruct the movement of his/her business affairs and to discover the acts computed in detriment to the creditors.

Documentation of business activities, although required for the protection of interests opposing those of entrepreneurs, is entrusted to the entrepreneurs themselves, without outside controls. The entrepreneur's compliance with the obligation to maintain book-keeping, and the truthfulness of the entries made are guaranteed only by the legislative provision of sanctions which, however, have effect in the event of the enterprise's judicial liquidation. Entrepreneurs who are declared bankrupt and found to have not maintained book-keeping over the three years preceding bankruptcy, or to have maintained irregular book-keeping, shall be punished for the crime of simple bankruptcy (Article 323 paragraph 2 of the Code of Crisis); bankrupt entrepreneurs who have destroyed or falsified book-keeping in order to obtain unfair profits for themselves or others, or to bring detriment to their creditors, or have kept the books in such a way as to make it impossible to reconstruct their capital or the movement of their business affairs, shall be punished for the crime of fraudulent bankruptcy (Article 322 paragraph 1 letter b) of the Code of Crisis).

The rules introduced with the Company Law Reform have broadened the scope for external supervision in accounting. Joint-stock companies that are making use of equity capital market and limited liability companies whose turnover and number of employees go beyond fixed thresholds have to nominate an external auditor.

70. The book-keeping that commercial entrepreneurs must practice is of two types: the day book and the inventory book (Article 2214 paragraph 1 of the Civil Code). They must furthermore practice the other forms of book-keeping required by the nature and size of the enterprise. Finally, for each business transaction, they must keep the originals of the letters, telegrams and invoices sent out (Article 2214 paragraph 2). The books must be conserved for ten years from the date of the last record. For the same period, the originals and copies of the letters, telegrams and invoices must also be kept (Article 2220).

Day books must indicate, day by day, the transactions relative to the operation of the enterprise (Article 2216). However, the entries do not necessarily have to regard each single transaction, but can globally regard the homogeneous transactions of a day.

Inventory books must contain the indication and evaluation of the credits and debts relative to the enterprise, as well as the credits and debts of the entrepreneur outside the enterprise. They must be compiled at the initiation of the enterprise's activity and every year subsequent (Article 2217 paragraph 1). Inventories must conclude with the balance sheet and with an account of the profits and losses, which must show the profits made and losses sustained (Article 2217 paragraph 2).

The 'other book-keeping' which, pursuant to Article 2214 paragraph 2, can be made compulsory on the basis of 'the nature or size of the enterprise' includes the ledger, in which individual transactions are recorded in relation to certain names and accounts, instead of in chronological order; the cash book, in which the income and outgo of money is recorded; and the store book, in which the income and outgo of goods, etc., are recorded.

All the above-mentioned records can be kept in both, paper or digital form. If kept in paper form, records may not be kept on loose sheets, but only in bound books, with each sheet glued to those directly preceding and following. This requirement does not apply to 'other book-keeping' referred to in Article 2214 paragraph 2: for these other forms, Article 2218 makes stamping and authentication merely facultative, thus showing that it is not compulsory to keep them in bound registers.

As far as the digital form is concerned, in order to be authentic, electronic documents have to be unmodifiable and marked by a digital signature. Moreover, in specific circumstances, they have to be validated by a public officer.

Chapter 5. Intangible Properties

§1. Company Names, Sign-Boards and Marks

71. Company names, sign-boards and marks together form the category of so-called distinctive signs: the first identifies the entrepreneur, the second the business, and the third the products which the entrepreneur puts on the market. They are referred to as intangibles and, similarly to material goods which are regulated in the third book of the Civil Code, they are the object of property rights and other rights. Distinctive signs have an important role in the relationships between entrepreneurs and consumers: they are 'customer collectors', in that they allow consumers to identify and distinguish between different entrepreneurs, their businesses and their respective products. They guarantee each entrepreneur the possibility to enjoy his/her own entrepreneurial success, with the exclusion of others.

72. Company names are the names under which entrepreneurs operate their business enterprises. They do not have to correspond to the real name of the entrepreneur: Article 2563, paragraph 2, states that company names may be 'formed in any way', thus satisfying the demand on the part of entrepreneurs to be identified by consumers, by a distinctive sign which is better suited for marketing and advertising than their real names. It is required, though, that company names 'however formed, must contain at least the surname or acronym of the entrepreneur' who originally formed the business, though not necessarily the surname or acronym of the entrepreneur currently operating it. Company names can be transferred, and the law exempts purchasers from having to add their own surname or acronym to the name purchased, and from mentioning the fact that the company name they use was transferred from someone else.

Every entrepreneur has 'the right to exclusive use of the company name chosen by him' (Article 2563 paragraph 1). The entrepreneur acquires his rights over the company name by simply using it, and the rights assume the characteristics of erga omnes rights: the entrepreneur who was the first to use a certain company name may demand that no other entrepreneur use a company name that is 'identical or similar', or which could 'create confusion as to the object of the business activity or the place where it is conducted' (Article 2564).

As a consequence of this right of the entrepreneur, every other entrepreneur is burdened with the obligation of differentiation: an identical or similar company name used subsequently by others 'must be integrated or modified by indications suitable to differentiate it' (Article 2564).

Article 2565 governs the transfer of company names: the first paragraph establishes that 'a company name cannot be transferred separately from the business'; the second paragraph adds that 'in the inter vivos transfer of a business, the company name does not pass to the purchaser without the consent of the assignor', thus showing that the transfer of a company name is an independent transfer, distinct from the transfer of the business; the last paragraph, relative to mortis causa succession in the business, provides for the automatic transfer of the rights to use of a company name, except when a will provides otherwise.

73. Sign-boards are the distinctive signs of businesses or of places of business. They perform the economic function of customer collecting, especially for those entrepreneurs who host consumers in their places of business (hotels, restaurants, stores of direct sale to the public).

Because the entrepreneur acquires the right to exclusive use of his sign-board, it must be distinctive: it must differentiate itself from the generic denomination of the business object.

Sign-boards can be a name or a design, or can consist of a linguistic expression or a device.

In Article 2568, the field of application of Article 2564 paragraph 1 is extended to sign-boards. Therefore a sign-board that is identical or similar to another sign-board used by a different entrepreneur, or which could cause confusion with respect to the object of the business enterprise or the place where it is operated, must be integrated or modified with indications suitable to differentiate it. Like the company name, the sign-board can be transferred only with the transfer of the business, but the assignor's consent to the transfer of the sign-board is not necessary.

74. Trademarks are the distinctive signs which entrepreneurs can affix, and generally do affix, to the products they put on the market (Article 2569). Trademarks can be affixed to the product by the manufacturer (factory marks), or by the retailer (commercial marks), who, however, cannot suppress the mark of the manufacturer (Article 2572). Apart from use by individual entrepreneurs, marks may be used by groups of entrepreneurs belonging to bodies or associations formed to guarantee the origin, nature or quality of certain products (collective marks, provided for by Article 2570 of the Civil Code and by Article 11 of Legislative Decree No. 30, 10 February 2005, so-called Industrial Property Code). In addition their use for distinguishing goods, trademarks can be used to distinguish, 'business activities of transport and communication, advertising, construction, insurance and credit, show business, radio and television, materials treatment and the like'.

Trademarks may consist in designs, composed of two-dimensional or three-dimensional devices, words or linguistic expressions. In any case, they must be distinctive. Therefore, they must be different from the generic denomination and descriptive indications of the product. When they are design marks, they must be different from designs imposed by the use or shape of the goods (Article 9 of the Industrial Property Code). If such distinctions were not required, the principle of freedom of competition would be altered: the exclusive use, on the part of an entrepreneur, of the generic denomination of a given product would give him/her a monopoly on that product. It is possible though to use as a mark a word resulting from a modification, even slight, of the generic denomination of the product, but in this case the mark enjoys limited protection (and for this reason is defined as a 'weak mark'): it is protected only to the degree in which it differs from the common denomination of the product.

The mark must furthermore meet the requirement of novelty: it must be different from designs and words already known as distinctive marks of products in the same category, manufactured or put on the market by others (Article 12 of the Industrial Property Code).

75. All entrepreneurs have the right to make exclusive use of the mark they have chosen for the products they produce or put on the market, or for the services they perform; they, therefore, enjoy an absolute right corresponding to the one they have on the company's name and sign-board.

Against counterfeiters, the entrepreneur may request an inhibitory action to prevent the counterfeiter from continuing to use the mark; an action of removal, ordering the destruction of the words or designs with which the counterfeit was committed and, if necessary to suppress the counterfeited mark, the destruction of the products on which the mark was affixed; and the payment of damages which the owner of the mark suffered as a result of the counterfeit (*see* Articles 124 et seq. of the Industrial Property Code).

The right to exclusive use of the mark can be acquired in two ways: either by obtaining a registration for the trademark, which is granted after an examination by the Italian Patent and Trade Mark Office is carried out to see that all the legal requirements have been fulfilled (registered trademarks: Article 2569 of the Civil Code), or by the entrepreneur's use of the mark independently from registration (unregistered trademarks: Article 2571 of the Civil Code). Unregistered trademarks enjoy weaker legal protection since their use can prevent third parties from registering an identical or similar mark, not satisfying the novelty requirement, only if they have become known throughout the entire national territory. If the unregistered trademark is known only locally, third parties can register an identical or similar mark. In such a case the party who used the unregistered mark may continue to use it, notwithstanding the registration obtained by others, but only within the limits of prior use, that is, within the local limits (Article 2571 of the Civil Code).

Those who distinguish their products with a non-registered trademark that does not have national recognition are exposed to the risk that third parties may use the same mark in other geographic areas, or that third parties may even obtain the registration. If this were to happen, they would not enjoy any legal protection for their mark if they tried to extend the market of the goods they produce from the local area to a larger area. On the other hand, by registering a mark the entrepreneur acquires the right to the exclusive use of that mark, even if use has not yet been commenced: pursuant to Article 20 of the Industrial Property Code, not only those who already use a mark can obtain its registration, but also those who propose to use one.

Registered marks are, moreover, protected in the entire national territory (or international territory, if the registration is carried out through the International Office in Geneva: Article 17 of the Industrial Property Code), even if they have not yet become known in that territory: their legal protection precedes their notoriety and thus allows entrepreneurs to invest vast amounts of capital in the advertising launch of new products and in the advertising launch of already existing goods in new markets.

Rights on registered trademarks last for ten years, but can be renewed at expiration for additional ten-year periods, for unlimited number of times (Article 16 of the Industrial Property Code).

Registration is forfeited if the mark is not used within five years of the date of the registration's grant or, in any case, if use is interrupted for five consecutive years (Article 24 of the Industrial Property Code). Furthermore the right to exclusive use of the mark is forfeited if it is ascertained that the mark has fallen into public domain (having become a generic denomination of the product) with the owner's acquiescence.

76. Just as firms and sign-boards, trademarks can be considered an autonomous asset which can be the object of trade: the mark used to distinguish a famous product is, in itself, a guarantee of profits and has, therefore, considerable value in trade. Also here, as in matters of firms and sign-boards, the interests of the entrepreneur in the trade of a mark are in contrast with need to protect consumers. For the protection of consumers, the Civil Code offers the provision of Article 2573, according to which 'the exclusive right to the use of a registered trademark can be transferred only with the business or a particular branch thereof'. In accordance with the second paragraph of the same Article, the transfer of the mark does not require, once the business has been transferred, a specific agreement.

77. In this regard, however, it should be noted that the above-mentioned discipline has undergone significant modifications with the enforcement in Italy of the provisions of European Economic Community (EEC) Directive No. 89/104 of 21 December 1988 harmonizing the legislation of the Member States on the subject of trademarks.

In fact, the principle of free transfer of the mark has been adopted, so that now assignment and licensing of marks may be carried out separately from the transfer of the relative business, the agreement of the owner being sufficient to finalize the contract.

The enactment of the EEC Directive, carried out with Legislative Decree No. 480 of 4 December 1992 has brought further important changes in this field:

(1) The revised law provides a broader definition of registrable signs; the only limitation being that the signs must be able to be represented graphically.
(2) It explicitly states that the right to exclusive use is incorporated in the right of the owner to prohibit third parties, save by his consent, from using a sign which is identical or similar to the registered mark, for identical or similar products or services in order to avoid the consequently possible creation of confusion on the part of the public, which may also consist in a risk of association of two signs.
(3) The principle of relativity is still valid in the protection provided for trademarks, so that the exclusive right to a mark extends only to those products or services which fall within its scope of use. However, the new law provides for a broader protection of marks that enjoy notoriety ('well-known' marks) vis-à-vis identical or similar marks distinguishing goods or services, even if dissimilar, if the use of those marks, without due cause, permits the taking of unfair advantage of the distinctive character and notoriety of the mark, or is detrimental to the owner.
(4) The principle of 'exhaustion of rights within the Community' is explicitly introduced, though in a modified form. An owner can oppose further commercialization in the national territory of products put on the EEC market, bearing

his mark, by the owner himself/herself or with his consent, only if he/she can demonstrate legitimate reasons, and in particular if the product has been altered or modified.

(5) A broader possibility of trademark ownership has been provided for so that marks may be registered by anyone, even non-entrepreneurs.

(6) The 'secondary meaning' theory has been explicitly recognized in its two-fold meaning of reinforcement and ex-novo acquisition of the distinctive character of a sign originally lacking it because it was generic or descriptive of the product which it distinguished. In both cases, the nullity of the mark is avoided.

(7) The so-called principle of uniformity of distinctive signs has been codified, according to which signs that were previously adopted as a firm, sign-board or company name, cannot be registered as marks, if, by virtue of the identity or similarity of the business activities of the owners of those signs, and the products or services for which the mark has been adopted, a risk of confusion can arise on the part of the public, which may also consist in a risk of association of different signs.

(8) A sanction has been provided for cases in which deceptive use of the sign directly affects the ownership of the right (previously the only available remedy was to prove that such behaviour was as an act of unfair competition).

(9) The 'subjective theory' of vulgarization has been put into force, according to which a trademark is forfeited if, as a result of the activity or inactivity of its owner, it has become the common name in the trade of the product or service.

§2. Intellectual Works and Industrial Inventions

78. Intellectual works are works of creative nature belonging to the sciences, literature, music, the figurative arts, theatre, cinema, etc. (Article 2575 of the Civil Code).

The category, since it comprises all intellectual creations, is extremely vast. The characteristic distinguishing it is the search for novelty in the various sciences and arts, novelty not conceived for a practical application.

Works of decorative nature, in which the search for expression is lacking, and works of ornamental nature (such as models and ornamental designs), in which the search for aesthetic novelty does exist, but is aimed at an immediate practical application, are not intellectual works.

Even websites benefit from the protection accorded to intellectual works: in particular, the Copyright Act (Law No. 633/1941) covers every single part of the site, either a text, an image, a music, a film or a photo.

79. The category of intellectual works extends to the limits of another category of intellectual creation: industrial inventions. These are technical inventions which have the characteristic of novelty and can be used for industrial applications, such as: (a) new processing methods, new machines and new instruments for production in general; (b) new industrial products; (c) technical applications of new scientific principles, provided they are created for immediate industrial results (Articles 2585 of the Civil Code and 45 of the Industrial Property Code).

Practically, in this matter we are dealing with technological innovations in industry, and new inventions are those that are not already comprised in the state of the art, or, that is, already accessible by the public through their description or use.

80. Similarly to distinctive signs, intellectual works and industrial inventions are considered intangibles. Creators are recognized two distinctive rights in regard to these intangibles: the moral right of the author or inventor and the patrimonial right.

The moral right is the right to the paternity of the work or invention or, rather, the right to be recognized as the creator. This right is indefeasible, irrevocable and non-transferable (Articles 2577, 2582 and 2589 of the Civil Code). After the death of the author, the right can be enforced by the spouse and children or, in their absence, by direct ascendants and descendants, independently of their hereditary quality, and without temporal limits.

The patrimonial right is the exclusive right to the economic exploitation of the work or invention. It is conceived of as an actual property right and it implies the right to enjoy and use it on an exclusive basis. Differently from the moral right, this right is transferable (Articles 2581 and 2589 of the Civil Code) and can be the object of contracts allowing others the exploitation of the work or invention, while the ownership of the moral right remains intact. Under this light, attention must be given to publishing agreements for intellectual works and licensing agreements for patents of inventions. Publishing agreements usually involve the transfer of the rights of utilization of the work which the editor undertakes to publish. The licensing agreement of a patent, on the other hand, is the contract by means of which the owner of the invention allows others the exclusive or non-exclusive use of the invention.

81. The rights on intellectual works and those on industrial inventions are acquired in different ways. The author derives his rights to the former at the very moment of creating the work (Article 2576 of the Civil Code). The inventor, on the other hand, only acquires his rights to the invention at the time he/she is granted the patent of the invention (Article 2584 of the Civil Code), with effects running from the date of application. From this it follows that among a number of creators of the same invention, the inventor who first applies to the National Patent and Trade Mark Office for a patent, is the one who acquires the moral and patrimonial rights to that invention. The Patent and Trade Mark Office grants patents for inventions upon verifying the correctness of the application and the industrial quality of that which is described as an invention. However, unlike other in countries, the Italian Patent and Trade Mark Office does not conduct any technical examination or search on the novelty of the invention. Therefore, the patent itself does not constitute a right, but only creates a presumption that the object of the patent is indeed an invention and that the owner of the patent is in fact the inventor, and, as a presumption, it can be overturned in court by contrary proof.

Methods for surgical, therapeutic and diagnostic treatment of the human and animal body cannot be patented, nor can the inventions whose realization would be contrary to public order or morality (Article 45 of the Industrial Property Code).

82. The right to the exclusive use of an intellectual work or industrial invention is not everlasting: copyrights last for seventy years after the death of the author, while patents of invention last for twenty years from the filing date of the application and can be forfeited earlier if the invention is not exploited within three years from the grant of the patent, or for failure to pay the annual tax on the patent.

The patent attributes the owner the exclusive right to realize the invention and to make profit from it in the State territory. The exclusive right obtained with a patent comprises, besides the manufacture of the product, also the sale of the product; the exclusive right on the sale is exhausted, however, once the product is put on the market.

Against those who illegally exploit the invention, the owner has the right to bring actions for patent infringement and for compensatory damages: the aim of the first action is to obtain a sentence to inhibit further illegal use of the invention, and to remove or destroy the means used for the infringement and the infringing products; with the second, the owner may request that the judge determine the amount of damages sustained also in relation to possible future infringements.

83. On 11 May 2018, the Legislative Decree No. 63 has been adopted, pursuant to Directive (EU) 2016/943, with the aim of protect undisclosed know-how and business information (i.e., trade secrets) against their unlawful acquisition, use and disclosure. In particular, Legislative Decree 63/2018 modifies both the Italian Code on Intellectual Property and the Italian Criminal Code in order to ensure an adequate protection to trade secrets, which are secret information with a specific commercial value.

With Law Decree 148/2017, the Italian legal system implemented the rules contained in Directive 26/2014, in order to improve the transparency of how 'collecting societies' operate and liberalize processes for licensing and transferring IP to allow for new types of contract.

84. On 17 May 2019, the European Parliament approved the Directive (EU) 790/2019, concerning copyright in the Digital Single Market, whose main goal is to further harmonize EU copyright law with particular laws on 'digital and cross-border uses of protected content'. It also deals with the improvement licensing practices and the ensuring of wider access to content.

85. Finally, utility models and design rights must be mentioned.

Utility models are minor inventions: they do not create a new machine or instrument of production, but confer already invented machines and instruments greater effectiveness or convenience of use. Those who obtain this type of patent have recognized rights similar to those of the inventor, with the difference that the economic right only lasts ten years and can be forfeited for non-use after a year from the grant of the patent.

Design rights are intellectual works applied to industry. Their function is to protect the form, line, colour or ornament of industrial products. Here also a patent can be obtained conferring a patrimonial right lasting fifteen years and a moral right.

The Italian government has implemented the EC Directive No. 98/71 by adopting Legislative Decree No. 95/2001, concerning industrial design and utility models. The new legislation changed the former rules with respect to both the prerequisite for protection and its scope. In order to obtain the protection granted by law the work shall have an individual character. Moreover, current rules allow for cumulation of both design and copyright protection.

Chapter 6. Judicial Liquidation

§1. Prerequisites for Judicial Liquidation

86. The legal system is institutionally organized to protect collective interests that may be damaged by a business crisis. The matter was disciplined by a special law contemporaneous with the Civil Code (Royal Decree No. 267 of 1942, the so-called Bankruptcy Law). Now, the legal framework concerning the crisis of enterprises has been significantly modified by legislative Decree No. 14 adopted on 12 January 2019, pursuant to enabling Law 155/2017, the so-called 'Code of crisis', that will enter into force on 1 September 2021, as provided by Law Decree No. 23/2020 (so-called '*Decreto Liquidità*'), converted into Law No. 40/2020, repealing Bankruptcy Law. Other procedures have been introduced, particularly through a comprehensive reform of Bankruptcy Law in 2006 (*see* Legislative Decree No. 5 of 9 January 2006) to adapt the need for protecting creditors and to that of avoiding the dissolution of the business enterprise caused by bankruptcy: these are arrangements with creditors and they too are disciplined by the bankruptcy law. As a result, bankruptcy tends more and more to be adopted only as an extreme remedy, especially for medium or medium-large enterprises.

87. Judicial liquidation has two prerequisites, one objective and one subjective. The first is established by Article 1 of the Code of Crisis: entrepreneurs who are in a state of insolvency shall be subject to bankruptcy. The law gives a definition of 'state of insolvency', qualifying an insolvent debtor as one who 'is no longer able to regularly satisfy his obligations', and specifically states that the insolvency 'demonstrates itself with default or other outside facts' (Article 2, paragraph 1, letter b). Therefore, if insolvency is the impossibility of the entrepreneur to regularly meet his obligations, default is one of the ways by which insolvency becomes apparent.

The subjective prerequisite for judicial liquidation is, according to Article 1 of the Code of Crisis, that the insolvent debtor must be a private commercial entrepreneur who does not classify as a small entrepreneur. The entrepreneur may be either an individual or a commercial company, thus excluding public economic entities, but including joint-stock companies which are held by the State.

The notion of small entrepreneur is contained in the Code of Crisis. Article 2, paragraph 1, letter d) states that those entrepreneurs who cumulatively hold in the three exercises before the instance of judicial liquidation is filed or, alternatively, the activity is started, the following prerequisites, are not subject to judicial liquidation proceedings:

(a) total assets below EUR 300,000 on an annual basis;
(b) gross revenues below EUR 200,000 on an annual basis;
(c) aggregate debts below EUR 500,000.

In addition, the judicial liquidation procedure cannot be declared against agricultural enterprises.

§2. The Judicial Liquidation Procedure

88. The opening of judicial liquidation procedure is declared by the court of jurisdiction, where the legal seat of the business enterprise is located. The proceeding may be initiated by the debtor himself/herself, one or more creditors, or the public prosecutor (Article 37 of Code of Crisis).

89. At this stage the proceeding is held to a standard of maximum speed. The court ascertains whether the prerequisites of the judicial liquidation have occurred and, if the court upholds the petition, it issues a sentence declaring the opening of the procedure (Article 44). This sentence includes the nomination of the delegated judge and the official receiver. It also requires the debtor to file the company's financial statements and books. In addition, it fixes a deadline before which creditors must file their application for admission to the proceeding and establishes the date of the hearing for the meeting of creditors.

During the proceeding the debtor is deprived of its assets.

90. Four bodies are appointed to carry out these procedures:

(a) the court, which appoints or dismisses the bodies of the proceeding and is authorized to decide any dispute that arises during the proceeding (Articles 122);
(b) the delegated judge, who directs the proceeding and oversees the conduct of the official receiver (Article 123);
(c) the official receiver, who becomes the administrator of the debtor's assets and performs all the activities of the procedure (Articles 125 et seq.);
(d) the committee of creditors, which is the self-governed body representing creditors. This committee is made up of three to five members appointed by the delegated judge. The committee controls the activity of the receiver, authorizes some acts and expresses opinions (Articles 138 and 1).

§3. Effects of Judicial Liquidation

91. The sentence declaring the opening of judicial liquidation has multiple consequences for the debtor and his creditors, as well as third parties in general.

For the debtor, the declaration of the opening of judicial liquidation produces two different sets of consequences.

Economic effects may be summarized in the so-called dispossession (Article 142): the debtor is deprived of the availability and management of his assets, which is performed by the official receiver.

Instead, other effects concern specific information obligations that shall be complied by debtor, such as the information relating to residence or domicile.

92. Pursuant to equal treatment under the law, the individual creditor is prohibited from commencing or pursuing separate executive actions against the bankrupt after the date of the declaration of the opening of judicial liquidation (Article 150).

From that date on, creditors can only have their debts satisfied through the procedure. Once their credits have been ascertained they become concurrent creditors. At this stage, *par condicio creditorum* is accomplished by distributing assets among creditors in proportion to the amounts of their respective credits. Among creditors, however, there is a fundamental difference in priority depending upon whether they are secured creditors, holding pledges, mortgages or liens on the assets of the debtor or unsecured creditors, known as simple creditors. The former has the right to preempt the assets, which are the object of their guarantee or security, and if the price obtained does not wholly fulfil their credit, they may concur with the unsecured creditors to divide the residual assets.

Contractual relationships involving the bankrupt, which are still pending on the date of the declaration of opening of judicial liquidation, can either be terminated or continued (*see* Articles 172 et seq.).

§4. The Crisis of Group of Business

93. The Code of Crisis takes into account the judicial liquidation of group of business. The procedure is unified, hence, it is allowed to:

- the submission of a single request to a single court, to be individuated according to the Centre of Main Interest (COMI) of the business that exercises management and coordination activity or, in lack, the court of the place where the business has the highest debt exposure;
- the appointment of a single delegated judge and a single receiver;
- the identification of a unique judicial liquidation program coordinated by the individual masses of creditors;
- the autonomy of the assets and liabilities relating to each company in liquidation.

In the event that one of the group companies is subject to judicial liquidation, the receiver has the duty to report the situation to the administrative and control bodies of the other companies, in order to urge them to ascertain the possible state of insolvency (Article 287).

In the case of crisis or insolvency requests is presented by a single company which is part to the group, the request shall:

- contain analytical information on the structure of the group and on the existing participatory constraints between the companies and the companies;
- indicate the register of companies in which publicity is carried out pursuant to Article 2497*bis* of the Italian Civil Code;
- be accompanied by the filing of the group consolidated financial statements if it has been drawn up.

However, the receiver may request the appropriate information about the generality of the actual holders of rights to shares or quotas to the public authorities and CONSOB (Article 289).

The receiver has the right to promote:

- actions aimed at achieving the declaration of ineffectiveness of deeds and contracts implemented in the five years preceding the filing of the judicial liquidation application that have had the effect of shifting resources to another company of the group with prejudice to the creditors without prejudice to the provisions of Article 2492 of the Italian Civil Code;
- claw-back action on acts completed after the filing of the request for the opening of judicial liquidation or pursuant to Article 166 paragraph 1 letter. a) and b), in the two years prior to the filing of the application or in the previous year in cases pursuant to Article 166, paragraph 1, letters c and d), pursuant to Article 290;
- liability actions pursuant to Article 2497 of the Italian Civil Code;
- complaint pursuant to Article 2409 of the Italian Civil Code towards the directors and statutory auditors of group companies not subject to judicial liquidation procedure (Article 291).

94. The new legislation also provides for the deferral of the credits that the company or the body or the natural person carrying out the activity of direction or coordination has towards the companies subject to direction and coordination or that these latter have towards them on the basis of relationships of financing contracts after the filing of the judicial liquidation application or in the previous year. The deferred credits are ineffective if they were reimbursed in the previous year by the application for the opening of the judicial liquidation except for the application of the Article 102 on pre-deductible loans from shareholders (Article 292).

§5. Conduct of Business by the Debtor

95. Article 211 of the Code of Crisis states that the opening of judicial liquidation does not prevent the possibility of continuing carrying out the activities related to the business of debtor, upon the condition that it would not damage the satisfaction of creditors' expectations.

In this regard, the committee of creditors shall be informed, on a quarterly basis, of the way in which the business is conducted.

The delegated judge, upon positive opinion expressed by the committee of creditors, may authorize the possibility to lease the business or a branch.

§6. Closing of Judicial Liquidation

96. The judicial liquidation proceeding is closed in the following cases: (1) absence of creditors' applications for admission to the proceeding before the deadline set in the sentence declaring the opening of judicial liquidation; (2) full payment of the debts; (3) final division of the assets; (4) futility of further prosecution as a result of insufficient assets (Article 233).

Upon the closure of the procedure, the four bodies (mentioned in paragraph 90) terminate their duties, and all the effects of judicial liquidation, on both the debtor and the creditors, cease (Article 236).

Judicial liquidation can be closed without having to proceed to the liquidation of the assets. The creditors and third interested parties can propose an agreement (Article 240), according to which the creditors are paid in a certain percentage of their credits, identifying the guarantees which will secure the payment. These proposals can also be made to secured creditors and provide for a partial payment. The only condition is that this payment cannot be less than the sum secured creditors can reasonably expect to be paid after the liquidation.

Even the debtor can propose such agreement, upon certain conditions:

(1) after one year from the sentence declaring the opening of the judicial liquidation;
(2) by two years from the court decree that enforced the passive state;
(3) in case the debtors' proposal provide assets that increase the value of the assets at least of 10%.

The reform has granted the debtor the so-called fresh start benefit. Article 278 allows for a complete removal of the debts eventually remaining after the closing of the judicial liquidation, provided that the debtor: (1) has cooperated with the bodies of the proceeding, giving them all the necessary information and documents; (2) has not delayed the proceeding; (3) has not benefited from fresh start twice in the past; (4) has not benefited from a 'fresh start' in the five preceding years; (5) has not distracted funds or increased the default or made the reconstruction of assets more difficult or made abusive recourse to bank credit; (6) has not been condemned for bankruptcy crimes or other economic crimes.

§7. Judicial Liquidation of Companies with Partners Having Unlimited Liability

97. In partnerships, both the company and the unlimited liable partners are qualified as entrepreneurs.

Pursuant to Article 1 of the Code of Crisis, entrepreneurs who carry on a commercial business activity are subject to judicial liquidation proceedings. Under Article 256, the sentence declaring the opening of judicial liquidation of a company with unlimited liable partners extends its effects to unlimited liable partners, or of all the partners in general partnerships and the general partners in limited partnerships. Therefore, the judicial liquidation of the company has as its object company assets, while the judicial liquidation of individual partners has as its object all personal assets of each of them (Article 258). The judicial liquidation of each unlimited liable partner is automatic, without the need to ensure that the prerequisites for judicial liquidation are present for each of them.

The same principle is also applicable to secret partners: after the declaration of the company's opening judicial liquidation, partners other than those already declared insolvent are discovered and the court declares them insolvent too, even if they are personally solvent (Article 256). This is also the case with secret companies.

§8. Early Warning

98. Articles 12 et seq. of the Code of Crisis deal with the mechanism of early warning and the assisted composition of crisis. In particular, the audit bodies of the company, the Italian Tax Authority and the Italian Institute for Social Security shall promptly point the clues of crisis, which are indicated as economic and financial imbalances, to be evaluated according to the characteristics of the company and the activity carried out. In such cases, the debtor can recourse to a specific body instituted in each Chamber of Commerce (the so-called OCRI, i.e., Organismo di Composizione della Crisi) in order to start a procedure of assisted composition of the crisis.

§9. Other Procedures

99. In addition to judicial liquidation, the Code of Crisis regulates compulsory liquidation, a substitute for judicial liquidation and arrangements with creditors.

Certain categories of entrepreneurs are subject to compulsory liquidation in the event of insolvency (Articles 193 et seq.). These categories are all subject to State surveillance, and include: banks, insurance firms, cooperatives and other categories indicated by specific laws.

While some enterprises are subject to both bankruptcy and compulsory liquidation (such as cooperatives pursuant to Article 2540 of the Civil Code), generally speaking, compulsory liquidation excludes the declaration of opening of the judicial liquidation. Consequently, the procedure begun first precludes the commencement of the other (Article 295).

100. Articles 84 et seq. of the Code of Crisis allow entrepreneurs who are in a state of crisis to propose creditors an arrangement with creditors based on a recovery plan that can provide (Articles 84 et seq.): (1) debts restructuring and satisfaction of creditors in any form (through the sale of goods or other extraordinary operations, the assignment of shares, bonds, warrants, etc.); (2) the assignment of the debtors' activity to an assignee. Creditors can be divided into classes. Each class can be treated differently according to the legal position or economic interests of creditors belonging to it. No minimum percentages of unsecured creditors' satisfaction are requested. The plan is, instead, to provide secured creditors a minimum level of satisfaction (they cannot receive less than they could reasonably expect in case of liquidation of the enterprise).

In order to be admitted to this procedure the debtor has to file a request to the court of the jurisdiction of his registered office. If the judge declares the arrangement admissible the debtor is allowed to continue to manage his enterprise, but subject to the surveillance of a judicial commissioner who is appointed by the judge. Extraordinary transactions require the approval of the judge. As for creditors, upon the authorization by the judge of the request of debtor, they cannot commence or proceed with restraining or enforcement actions on the assets of the debtor (so-called automatic stay).

If the proposal for an agreement is refused, the court, can no more declare the opening of judicial liquidation, unless creditors expressly require it or there is a request from the public prosecutor. If the agreement is declared admissible by the judge all creditors are bound by it. Finally, payments made according to the agreement cannot be the object of a claw-back action in case the arrangement fails and the judicial liquidation is declared open.

The Code of Crisis stresses, in particular, the arrangement with creditors enabling the business continuity, because it is finalized to re-admit the enterprise to the market, even allowing the lease of business in case it could be useful to the business continuity. The satisfaction of debts shall mainly derive from the business activity.

The Code even introduced the arrangement with creditors in case of group of business.

101. The reform has also provided for two forms of out-of-court agreements: debt-restructuring agreements and recovery plans.

Debt-restructuring agreements are regulated by Articles 57 et seq. of the Code. They can be entered into by the entrepreneur in a state of crisis and creditors representing 60% of all claims. No judicial commissioner can be appointed although the agreement is subject to judicial approval. In order to be approved the agreement must be accompanied by an expert report, stating the feasibility of the agreement. After the approval the agreement is published in the Registry of Enterprises. Unlike pre-bankruptcy agreements, debt-restructuring agreements only bind participating creditors. As well as in case of arrangement with creditors, the automatic stay is allowed upon request of debtor and authorization of the judge, for a maximum duration of twelve months. Payments made according to them are not subject to claw-back actions.

The Code introduces the instrument of facilitated debt-restructuring agreement, that can be entered into by entrepreneurs and creditors representing 30% of all claims.

Even for the debt-restructuring agreements, the Code of Crisis introduced a specific regulation for group of business.

102. Recovery plans are considered by the Code of Crisis, which grants protection from claw-back actions (Article 166, paragraph 3, letter d). Such agreements between the debtor and some of his creditors may provide for new finance (credit or risk capital) and/or for the rescheduling of debts. In order to avoid claw-backs, the agreement must be based on a recovery plan, whose reasonableness must be stated by a professional auditor. The plan has to ensure the recovery of the debt exposure and the re-balancing of the financial situation of the debtor.

103. Legislative Decree No. 270/1999 provides for a special procedure for large insolvent companies (special administration), as an alternative to bankruptcy. This procedure aims at the reorganization of insolvent corporations by restructuring business or transferring assets to other companies.

Since 2003, on the occasion of some huge company defaults, some special laws have been adopted providing for some special administration procedures for big corporations in financial distress (*see* Law No. 39 of 18 February 2004 and Law No.

166 of 27 October 2008). These laws aimed at introducing innovative legal instruments for recovering companies, whose defaults would have had a significant economic and social impact. Some of the novelties introduced by these reforms have been absorbed by the Bankruptcy Law Reform of 2006.

§10. Bank Recovery and Resolution

104. In the aftermath of 2007 financial crisis, the European Union adopted the 2014/59/EU Directive, also known as Bank Recovery and Resolution Directive (BRRD), that has been implemented in Italy through Legislative Decrees Nos 180–181 dated 16 November 2015, with the aims of: (a) preventing the insolvency; and (b) in case of insolvency, reducing the negative effects, by protecting the functions of the bank that have a systemic role.

In particular, the BRRD and the Italian legislative decrees provide:

(a) recovery plans, which are preventive measures that fall within the prudential governance; the content of recovery plans shall be determined by the competent resolution authority (i.e., the Bank of Italy in case of subjects with legal seat in Italy);
(b) resolution measures, such as the bail-in, which is the reduction or the conversion in equity of the creditors' and shareholders' rights;
(c) special administration, in case of material violation of laws, regulation or articles of association, or in case of material worsening of the situation of the bank or of the group, or in case of severe loss;
(d) compulsory liquidation, in case of distress.

Chapter 7. Paper Titles

§1. Notion and Function of Paper Titles

105. The notion of paper titles comprises a great variety of documents from bills of exchange to checks, from company stocks and bonds to consolidated annuities and documents of title to goods.

The economic purpose of these titles is to circulate movables either directly (with the transfer of money, credit and goods) or indirectly, by circulating documents that represent movable property, and thus make the latter quicker and safer to circulate. Bills of exchange, checks and stocks are moveable properties (Article 812): their right to be so is stated on the document and is incorporated in the document as a movable property, so that it functions as a vehicle of this stated right. It follows then that the right circulates, not by its own rules of circulation, but according to those of the document in which it is incorporated and therefore, by the less strict rules which govern the circulation of movable properties. At the same time, the restrictions on this right (lien, seizure and foreclosure) must be carried out on the title, and have no effect if they are not apparent from the title (Article 1997).

Among the various types of paper titles, the most common are those documents which state a credit and, in particular, the right to the payment of the sum of money indicated therein. Bills of exchange, checks, company bonds and consolidated annuities have these characteristics.

Other titles exist which represent a more complex legal situation, such as company stocks, which represent the quality of partner or the position as part of the company contract.

In other titles, such as documents of title to goods, a credit is still represented, but for the delivery of the indicated goods rather than for the payment of a sum of money.

106. The essence of the paper title is in the fact that the right to the payment of a sum of money or to the consignment of goods circulates according to the rules for circulation of movable properties, rather than the more complex and less secure rules governing the transfer of credits (Articles 1260 et seq.). Furthermore, the status of partner in a joint-stock company also circulates according to the rules of circulation of movable properties, instead of those regarding the transfer of contracts (Articles 1406 et seq.).

The following sequence, therefore, applies: (a) attaining possession of the title produces the original acquisition of the property and this fact is independent of whether the former possessor was the owner (this principle is called the principle of autonomy and is provided by Article 1994 of the Civil Code); (b) the acquisition of the property of the title implies acquiring the ownership of the right indicated therein. It also determines the original acquisition of the title, so that the principles of the transfer of credits are overcome: those who are debtors on the basis of a paper title can, in fact, legitimately refuse to pay the credit if the title does not meet the legal requirements, if obstacles arise from the literal context of the title, or if their signature has been forged, if they were incapacitated at the time of issue of the title, if the conditions provided by the law to carry out the judicial action are lacking or if personal relationships exist with those requesting payment of the title (this represents the principle of literariness versus abstraction, provided by Article 1993 of the Civil Code); (c) attaining the title, by its own rules of circulation, implies the acquisition of the so-called legitimation, that is, it entitles the assignee to ask for payment of the sums indicated on the title without needing to furnish proof of having legitimately attained possession of the document. The debtor who refuses to pay the sums indicated in the title bears the burden of proving that the person requesting the payment is not the real creditor.

§2. Circulation

107. The title can be transferred in various ways according to whether it is a bearer bond, an order bond or a nominative bond. Bearer bonds can be transferred by simply consigning the document (as with company bonds). Order bonds are transferred with the consignment of the document and the endorsement (for instance checks and bills of exchange). Nominative bonds are transferred through the consignment of the document with annotations both on the title and on the register of the issuer (e.g., company stocks).

108. The holder of the bearer bond is entitled to exercise the right indicated in the bond by simply presenting the bond to the debtor (Articles 1993 and 2003, paragraph 2, of the Civil Code). These are essentially the titles issued in series, such as consolidated annuities, stocks and company bonds. In this connection, the principle of free issue does applies: new paper titles not provided by the law can be created. However, the issue of bearer bonds, which incorporate the obligation to pay a sum of money, is permitted only in the cases decided by the law (Article 2004) since circulating these bonds assumes a function similar to that of money circulation.

109. It is characteristic of order bonds that their circulation must be documented on the title through endorsement by the previous possessor to the subsequent one, who is entitled to exercise the rights indicated in them thanks to an uninterrupted series of endorsements.

Order bonds include bills of exchange, checks and titles that are unconnected by a series to individual credit operations. The endorsement is the order formulated on the back of the order bond by the endorser to the debtor, to perform the obligation in favour of the new payee of the title (the endorsee). The endorsement can be 'special', that is it may indicate the endorsee, or 'blank' and bear only the signature of the endorser without the name of the endorsee (Article 2009, paragraph 2). Order bonds with blank endorsements can be successively circulated without being documented, much like bearer bonds (Article 2011, paragraph 2), but one of the successive bearers of the order bond can fill in the endorsement with their own name and newly endorse the order bond, to ensure the continuity of the endorsements.

110. With nominative bonds, the possession of the bond must be further qualified by the indication of the name of the possessor on the bond and in the issuer's register. As with bearer bonds, these are titles issued in series, like consolidated annuities, stocks and company bonds, which must be registered in the consolidated annuities register, in the shareholders register and in the register of debenture holders.

111. The entitlement for these bonds can be obtained in one of three ways. Article 2022 gives two of these: through annotation by the issuer of the name of the purchaser on the bond and in the register; through issue by the issuer of a new bond registered to the purchaser and subsequent annotation of the issue in the register. However, Article 2023 provides the most frequently used way: the bond is transferred by means of an endorsement, necessarily naming the endorsee, which must be authenticated by a notary public or stockbroker; the endorsee, who demonstrates his possession on the basis of a series of uninterrupted endorsements, then has the right to obtain annotation of transfer in the issuer's register.

112. Paper titles are distinct from legitimation documents and quasi titles. Legitimation documents have the sole function of identifying the party with the right to a certain service (e.g., a railway ticket), while quasi titles are only to simplify the transfer of credit without, however, applying the above-mentioned principles (e.g., money orders).

§3. Abstract and Special Titles

113. Abstract titles, like bills of exchange and checks, do not make any mention of the reason for their issue; they are considered independently from the cause underlying the transaction.

The literalness of the title is related to its abstraction: the possessor can make it valid only according to its literal contents, without reference to facts or circumstances not mentioned on the title, and the debtor can oppose the possessor on only 'exceptions based on the literal context of the title' (Article 1993).

With the issue of an abstract title the obligatory relationship is doubled: to the underlying obligation, which survives the issue of the title (Article 66 of Royal Decree No. 1669 of 14 December 1933, of the law on bills of exchange), is added a distinct parallel obligation incorporated in the title and defined as a paper right. The following connection exists between the two obligations: (a) as long as the paper right can be exercised, the underlying right is suspended; (b) the satisfaction of the paper right, that is, the payment of the bill of exchange or the check, automatically extinguishes the underlying right.

114. Special titles are paper titles that indicate the special cause of the relationship upon which the issue of the title is based: consolidated annuities and company bonds, behind which are specific lending operations; company stocks, which represent the quality of partner in the company issuing them; also documents of title to goods, such as certificates of deposit (deposit warrant and warehouse warrant), which indicate a deposit contract, as well as way-bills (bills of lading and duplicates of consignment notes), which mention a conveyance contract.

In these cases there is no paper right other than the special one, since the title incorporates the same special right. Important consequences are derived from this during circulation. Even if the special title is that of an original acquisition like any other paper title, the purchaser of the property of the document also purchases the ownership of the right originating from the specific cause the document mentions. Thus, the debtor can always oppose the absence of the obligatory relationship that originated the issue of the title, not only with the first payee but with all the successive owners as well.

Furthermore, these titles lack literalness: the debtor can oppose all successive owners not only on the exceptions based on the literal content of the title, but also on those based on the contract underlying the issue of the same title.

§4. Company Shares

115. As pointed out above, company shares are the minimum fraction of the capital stock of a company that must be purchased in order to become a stockholder in a company or partnership limited by shares (Articles 2346–2362 of the Civil Code). They are represented by a document that has the nature of paper titles, and that attributes the quality of shareholder to the persons who purchase them according to predetermined rules of circulation (*see* paper titles).

116. Shares can be nominative or to the bearer: while the latter are transferred with the consignment of the share, the former are transferred in different ways, the most common being the endorsement of the title authenticated by a public notary or by a stockbroker, followed by its annotation in the register of shareholders kept by the company. The purchaser of the title is entitled to exercise the rights of a shareholder if he/she demonstrates his/her possession of the title on the basis of an uninterrupted series of endorsements.

In Italy, it is required that shares be nominative; savings shares, introduced in 1974 as shares not entitling the right to vote, are an exception to this rule and can be bearer shares.

117. Rules concerning the circulation of shares only partially reflect the principles related to circulation of paper titles.

Law 289 of 19 June 1986, previously in force, setout rules to govern a system for the centralized administration of securities. The system applied only to securities listed on a stock exchange (thereby obliging intermediaries dealing in them to belong to the system) and to other unlisted securities widely distributed among the investing public. The system was a book-entry procedure where all transfers of securities took place without the actual physical movement of the certificates.

Legislative Decree No. 58/98 changed the system. The centralized administration of securities is now entrusted exclusively to specialist centralized securities depositories (società di gestione accentrata), which must be authorized by the CONSOB in agreement with the Bank of Italy.

Moreover, a system of compulsory dematerialization of paper titles has been introduced by Legislative Decree 213/1998. According to the new system shares traded on a stock exchange or widely distributed among the public cannot be represented by share certificates.

The certificates must, therefore, be cancelled and returned to the company that issued them. The issue and transfer of dematerialized shares take place solely through the centralized depository system. When issuing new shares, a company simply notifies the central depository of the total amount of the issue and the intermediaries to which the shares are to be credited. The intermediaries then register the shares in separate accounts for each shareholder. Shares can only be transferred through authorized intermediaries, who must register the transaction in customers' accounts once it has been completed.

Chapter 8. The Stock Exchange: Stockbrokers – Movables Brokerage Firms

§1. The Stock Exchange as a Financial Market

118. The stock exchange is a market organized for the negotiation of fungible titles. In particular, the object of negotiations are titles of: (1) public and private debts of the issuer as well as annuities, redeemable shares, treasury bills, bonds; (2) property stocks of the companies issuing them.

Negotiations take place on the stock exchange regard securities which are already in circulation. Price lists indicate quotations taken from the demand and supply of the single values. Consequently they shift, sometimes considerably, from the conditions at which the securities were traded at the time of their initial public offer.

In the case of shares, prices on the stock exchange may not refer precisely to their intrinsic value (which can be estimated on the basis of the value on the balance sheet, the patrimonial content or the accumulation of earnings), stock exchanges represent prices and not valuations.

The Italian stock market is organized and managed by Borsa Italiana S.p.A. and was founded in 1997 following the privatization of the exchange. Borsa Italiana's primary objective is to ensure the development of the managed markets, maximizing their liquidity, transparency and competitiveness.

Borsa Italiana S.p.A. determines the types of exchange contracts admitted and is responsible for:

- defining and organizing the functioning of the markets;
- defining the rules and procedures for admission and listing on the market for issuers and brokers;
- managing and overseeing the market;
- supervisioning listed companies' disclosure.

In its current privatized structure Borsa Italiana is outlined as a market-management body endowed with operational autonomy and flexibility.

§2. Controls

119. The institutional framework within which the activities related to the movables market take place is represented in Italy by Law No. 272/1913 (modified by Decree No. 815 of 1923) and by the laws that were passed in the following years. Particularly, Law No. 216 of 7 June 1974 introduced many innovations regarding the supervision of the stock exchange activity and instituted the CONSOB, whose activities and competences have already been described in Chapter 3.

120. The new provisions contained in Legislative Decree No. 58/1998 (Consolidated Law on Financial Intermediation) broadened the supervisory and investigative powers of CONSOB and the Bank of Italy. The two institutions are also entitled to issue regulations on the functioning of the markets.

The Consolidated Law on Financial Intermediation and the implementing regulations issued by CONSOB and the Bank of Italy have contributed to enhance the competitiveness of Italy's markets and companies and have laid the foundations for the specification of a model of Corporate Governance in line with those of the countries with the most developed financial systems.

The supervisory powers of the authorities have been strengthened. The Bank of Italy and CONSOB, within the scope of their respective authority, may order the suspension or temporary limitation of the issue or redemption of units or shares of collective investment undertakings. Moreover, they are empowered to carry out inspections of authorized persons and require the exhibition of documents and the adoption of measures which are deemed necessary.

§3. Stock Exchange Contracts

121. Exchange contracts are those contracts whose object is the purchase or sale of government securities, shares, bonds and other securities issued in series and admitted to the stock exchange or the unlisted market (a market with simpler rules of operation in which securities often destined to the official market are negotiated). Except for the particular contract called the continuation note, the Civil Code does not specifically regulate exchange contracts: their discipline is laid down mainly by customs and practices of the stock exchange.

On the Italian stock exchange two types of contracts are used: spot contracts (otherwise known as cash basis deliveries), which are typical of bonds, and whose obligations have to be performed within three days of the stipulation; future contracts, which are typical of stocks, and provide for a deferred performance of the obligations of the contract.

Option contracts are also stock exchange contracts. Their object is represented by an option to purchase or sell a fixed amount of stocks at a certain price: the payment of the option is the sale price of the option and is always owed, unless the option is renounced.

§4. Floor Traders: Stock Brokers and Financial Intermediaries

122. Only qualified people can operate as intermediaries on the stock exchange. Traditionally these were stock brokers, defined as commercial traders, who worked on the stock exchange as authorized mediators in the negotiation of stock on behalf of their clients. Stock brokers, therefore, negotiated on behalf of third parties, who confer their orders to buy or sell; they were instead prohibited from operating for themselves and also, to further guarantee their professional independence, from conducting incompatible activities (e.g., company management).

123. With Law No. 1 of 2 January 1991, the category of stockbrokers was abolished, movables brokerage firms were regulated in order to operate as intermediaries for negotiations on the stock exchange.

Legislative Decree No. 58/1998 has considerably broadened the number of operators who may act as intermediaries within financial markets. The intermediaries who are authorized to operate on national markets can be differentiated according to their legal status, the geographical location of the access to the market, the type of activity performed on the market. Authorized intermediaries can play an active role in the price formation process as regards, both their own orders and orders made on behalf of their customers.

In accordance with the rules on trading services and recognition of foreign intermediaries provided by Legislative Decree No. 58/98 and set forth by Borsa Italiana, the following operators may request authorization to trade:

- individual stockbrokers, banks, Italian Securities Investment firms (SIM – Società di intermediazione Mobiliare), EU and non-EU investment companies, financial intermediaries complying with rules set forth in the Consolidated Banking Law (Legislative Decree No. 385/1993);
- local financial salesmen, with registered office in one of the countries of the EU, if they are subject to supervision by a public authority. There are special requirements concerning capital, respectability and professionality of such operators to ensure their reliability;
- non-EU banks and investment companies authorized to perform trading services for their own and customer account.

CONSOB has issued secondary legislation on intermediaries shortly after the adoption of Legislative Decree No. 58/1998. The secondary legislation on intermediaries, contained in the regulation approved by Resolution No. 20307 of 15 February 2018 completed the transposition into the Italian legal framework of the EU Directive 2014/65/EU ('Markets in Financial Instruments Directive' – MiFID II) and of the EU Regulation 600/2014 ('Markets in Financial Instruments and amending Regulation' – MiFIR).

The Regulation deals, in particular, with:

- the authorization of Italian Securities Investments Firm (SIM) and the entry into Italy of EU and non-EU investment firms other than banks;
- the disclosure obligation that the intermediaries shall comply within providing investment services;
- the evaluation of the clients according to adequacy, appropriateness and execution only;
- product governance;
- procedures aimed at ensuring correctness and transparency in providing investment services;
- provision of collective asset management and commercialization of open-end-funds (OICR).

In 2007, the European Parliament and the European Council adopted the Shareholder Rights Directive (SHRD) to ensure a better protection of the exercise of rights of shareholders in listed companies. In 2017, the revised Shareholder Rights

Directive (SHRD II), amended the SHRD aiming at encouraging long-term engagement of EU listed companies' shareholders. To achieve this long-term investment objective, the SHRD II describes new obligations for EU listed companies, intermediaries, institutional investors, asset managers and proxy advisors leading to a greater transparency regarding the investment strategy, the directors' remuneration, the voting process in general meetings, and the shareholders themselves.

The dispositions of the SHRD II pursue five main objectives leading to different types of obligations:

– ensuring that all investors are incentivized to participate in the long run to the life of companies in which they invest in order to make a more long-term sustainable EU economy;
– easing the identification of the shareholders by calling on intermediaries to communicate information regarding shareholders upon company's request (name, contact, registration number, number of shares);
– improving involvement of shareholders in corporate governance by calling on companies to provide their shareholders with means to vote on general meetings;
– encouraging transparency in the investment strategy by calling on institutional investors and asset managers to disclose relevant information;
– influencing directors' remuneration by involving the shareholders in the process of establishing, voting and publishing remuneration policies and reports on their implementation.

§5. Bonds

124. Along with shares, companies can also issue bonds, that can be sold and purchased in the Stock Market.

A corporate bond is a debt security issued by a corporation and sold to investors. The backing for the bond is usually the payment ability of the company, which is typically money to be earned from future operations. In Italy, Article 2412 of the Italian Civil Code sets forth a limit for the issuance of bonds by a company: the bonds issued, that can be registered or bearer, cannot overcome a threshold represented by the sum of twice the amount of share capital of the issuing company, of the legal reserve and of the available reserves as attested by the last approved financial statements. This threshold can be exceeded in case, for example, of debt securities issued in favour of professional investors or if the bonds are covered by mortgage on immovable properties of the company.

Even SRL can issue bonds, pursuant to Article 2483 Civil Code, that are called debt securities. Debt securities differ from the bonds issued by the Spa, in that, for the latter, the issue is provided for by law within certain limits, while in the SRL the issue of debt securities is permitted without limits only if provided for by the deed of incorporation. In addition, the bonds can be registered or bearer and freely placed on the market, while debt securities shall be only registered and can only be subscribed by professional investors.

§6. Crowdfunding

125. After the 2008 US subprime crisis, borrowers suffered from the credit crunch and dramatically reduced the access to credit, in particular SMEs in Italy, that usually rely on bank loans. Therefore, alternative funding instruments became necessary.

Within the number of alternative funding tools, significant success has gained crowdfunding, which can be defined as the financing of a project or a venture by a group of individuals instead of professional parties; it is usually realised through online campaigns, with relatively modest contributions from a large group of individuals, rather than seeking substantial sums from a small number of investors.

Crowdfunding can involve different form of activities, conventionally distinguished on the basis of the contribution made by the crowd:

(1) donation-based crowdfunding, typically used for charity or other socially relevant initiative; in such case, the contributor did not require nor expect a financial return;
(2) lending crowdfunding, also known as peer-to-peer (P2P) lending, which is a practice of debt financing that allows to lend money to individuals or businesses through online services that match lenders with borrowers without a financial institution working as an intermediary;
(3) reward-based crowdfunding, in which the funders receive non-financial awards in return of their contribution;
(4) equity crowdfunding; in this case, users invest in a start-up and receive shares in return. Investors become shareholders of the company.

126. Italy has been the first mover in regulating crowdfunding in the European Union context.

In fact, Italy has disciplined equity crowdfunding in 2012, when, through the Law Decree No. 179 of 18 October 2012, modifying the Consolidated Law on Finance, allowed innovative start-up companies to publicly offer shares on authorised Internet platforms. With the Law No. 33 of 24 March 2015, the provisions concerning equity crowdfunding have been extended to a broader category of firms, called 'Innovative Small Medium Enterprises'; thus, Italy restricts the field of application of equity crowdfunding exemptions to certain category of companies.

Crowdfunding has been disciplined even by a Consob Regulation 18592/2013, modified with Resolution 21110, issued on 18 October 2019, which transpose into the regulation the outcome of the consultation with the market. In particular, the Resolution has extended the access to crowdfunding even to bonds and debt securities issued by SMEs.

Chapter 9. Contracts for Entrepreneurial Activities

§1. General Principles

127. Unlike the Commercial Code of 1882, the Italian system no longer provides for a law of obligations and contracts applicable only to entrepreneurs.

The Civil Code of 1942, currently in force, unified the system of private law and provided for a unique discipline notwithstanding the qualifications of the parties.

The only exception to this rule is constituted by the provisions on the subject of representation. According to the general principles of the fourth book of the Civil Code, the fact that a party handles, by charge of another party, the business affairs of the latter does not, in itself, imply that the former is his representative. In fact, where by a special authorization by the concerned party, the appointment of an agent (Article 1392), giving another party power to act in his name with third parties is necessary, neither a mandate nor a work contract is sufficient to grant representative power.

On the subject of commercial enterprises, such principles lose their place to others that make it safer for third parties to deal with representatives of entrepreneurs (therefore, making the conclusion of deals quicker and safer). In these matters a special system of representation is applicable, according to which certain collaborators of commercial entrepreneurs (e.g., managers, head of business units, sales assistants, etc.) are, by the nature of their duties, given representative power: those acting in relationships with third parties through one of these positions are necessarily endowed with representative power, and those negotiating with them do not have the burden of verifying the existence of, or possible limits to, that power (Articles 2203 et seq. of the Civil Code).

§2. Sales Contracts

128. Sales contracts are the most important means through which the circulation of wealth occurs. They have as their object either the transfer of a material property or the transfer of a right or a contract (Article 1470 of the Civil Code).

Sales contracts produce real effects, in the sense that the property or the right is transferred from the seller to the purchaser by consent at the time of conclusion of the contract, and independently from the consignment of the object. It also produces obligatory effects: it imposes on the purchaser the obligation to pay the price, on the seller to consign the object and guarantee the purchaser against unapparent faults of the object and possible claims of third parties claiming ownership.

The sale, however, has only obligatory effects, and the transfer of the property of the sold object is not an immediate consequence of the contract, but occurs subsequently in the following cases: (1) the sale of objects determined only in their genre: here the property is transferred only when the goods are identified; (2) the sale of future goods not existing at the conclusion of the contract: the property is transferred when the goods come into existence; (3) the sale of goods owned by other parties: the property is transferred when the seller obtains the ownership of these goods; (4) sales in instalments with reservation of property: the purchaser becomes the owner only when and if the last instalment is paid.

129. Particular provisions regarding the sale of real estate properties. They can be sold by unit of measurement (for which the price is determined by a certain amount for each unit of measurement) or by the whole (the price is determined in relation to the entire property and not on the basis of its precise size). In the latter case, even if the size of the real estate property is indicated in the contract, the price cannot be raised or lowered unless the actual measurement is lesser or greater by at least a twentieth of that indicated.

The sale of movables can be carried out with a guarantee of satisfaction, upon trial or on documents: the sale is concluded respectively when satisfaction is communicated if the object in question is found to have the approved qualities, or by consignment of the document of title.

130. Article 23 of the Law Decree No. 133/2014, expressly disciplines the rent-to-buy contract. It is a new contractual model, considered to be a sort of merge between lease contract and sale contract: in fact, it provides the immediate use of immovable goods, according to the lessee the right to purchase the good within a certain term, allocating a part of the lease fee to the purchase price.

131. In 2002, a discipline concerning the sale of consumer goods has been adopted. Legislative Decree No. 24/2002, implementing EC Directive No. 44 of 25 May 1999 concerning 'certain aspects of the sale of consumer goods and associated guarantees', introduced Articles from 1519*bis* to 1519*nonies* to the Civil Code, now absorbed in the Code of Consumers, adopted by Legislative Decree No. 206 of 6 September 2005.

The scope of these rules is limited to sale, exchange, supply contracts and any other contract whose purpose is the supply of consumer goods. These rules only apply when the parties involved are the seller and the consumer.

The contracting goods are tangible movable items. The main purpose of the discipline is to enhance protection of consumer rights: the Code, on the one hand provides for a wider definition of faults, thus implying a broader liability of the seller, and on the other hand strengthens enforcement remedies.

§3. Other Contracts

I. Contracts for Distribution of Products: Estimation Contracts, Supply Contracts, Sales Licenses and Franchising

132. The distribution of products in the market, especially when dealing with mass production on a large scale, requires complex and thorough organization. Thus, a specific entrepreneurial activity dealing with the intermediation in the circulation of goods has developed and operates in the purchase and resale from the manufacturer to the wholesaler, from the wholesaler to the retailer and, finally, from the retailer to the consumer. The main risk of distribution is the risk of unsold goods, which is transferred from the manufacturer to the retailer because of sale contracts. Estimation contracts allow for a different allocation of the risk, by placing it on the manufacturer and releasing the retailer. Estimation contracts are the contracts by which one party transfers to the other one or more movable properties, and the other can, within an agreed-upon term, either pay the price or return the goods (Article 1556). The party transferring the goods remains their owner, but cannot sell them; those receiving the goods, although not the owner, can sell them (Article 1558). If at the end of the agreed-upon term, the latter have sold the goods, they pay the price; otherwise they return the goods, thus releasing themselves from the risk of the unsold goods.

133. Supply contracts are those contracts through which one party assumes the obligation to periodically or continuously supply goods to the other party for an agreed-upon price (Article 1559).

If the quantity to be supplied is not indicated in the contract, the rule according to which the supplier provides quantities of goods corresponding to the normal needs of the recipient party applies (Article 1560). The price, if not established in the contract, is determined according to the provisions disciplining sales and is paid, when dealing with periodic supply, at the time of each individual consignment, or at the expiration of use, when dealing with continuous supply.

In supply contracts between manufacturers and retailers, the first agrees to supply the latter on a continuous basis. Often an exclusivity clause in favour of the supplier (Article 1567), the buyer (Article 1568) or in favour of both is provided. In the first case, the retailer agrees to sell only the products of the manufacturer, excluding all similar products produced by others. In the second case the retailer obligates the manufacturer-supplier not to sell, either directly or indirectly, to others in the area assigned to the retailer.

134. From the supply contract between manufacturer and retailer with exclusivity in favour of the manufacturer, a different contract may originate: the sales license. The manufacturer-supplier undertakes to supply the retailer (licensee) the quantity of goods he/she needs, and he/she, in return, undertakes to order a minimum quantity, agreed upon in advance, and to carry out sales in a fixed area. This sales license is characterized by additional clauses which impose on the retailer internal rules for the organization of the enterprise, means of sale of the goods, and the sale price.

135. The involvement of the producer in the enterprise of the retailer is further demonstrated in another type of atypical contract: franchising. In this contract, the producer (franchisor) is the developer of a marketing plan for his own products, while the retailer (franchisee) is the mere executor of the plan established in all its details by the franchisor, and presents himself/herself to the public with the same entrepreneurial image as the franchisor.

II. Contracts for the Promotion of Business: Mediation, Agency and Commission

136. Enterprises engaged in the production or sale of goods or services often have an internal organization for the promotion of sales made up by their own employees specifically assigned to this activity. However, it frequently happens that enterprises hire external intermediaries who, acting as auxiliary entrepreneurs according to Article 2195, promote the conclusion of business transactions. The main types disciplined by the Civil Code are those of the mediator and the commercial agent.

137. Mediators are defined by Article 1754 as those who bring two or more parties together for the conclusion of a deal, without being related to any of them by relationships of collaboration, employment or representation. They are compensated with commission, which are paid by each of the parties, and only if the deal is concluded; otherwise they have only the right to a refund of the expenses sustained (Articles 1755 and 1756). The essential characteristic of mediators is that their position is independent and impartial with respect to the parties that they bring together: notwithstanding the charge assumed, mediators retain full liberty of action and are incentivized to promote deals only by the interest in collecting the commission.

Professional mediators must keep a special book, in which they must annotate the contracts stipulated through their mediation. They must also enrol in a special register kept by the Chambers of Commerce, the penalty for non-compliance being the loss of their right to the commission.

138. Commercial agents are different from mediators mainly in that their position is not characterized by independence and impartiality; they are also different in that their charge or assignment is stable, rather than occasional, as is the case with mediators.

With the agency contract an agent assumes the stable job of promoting the conclusion of contracts in a certain area for a certain principal (Article 1742). He/she has a stable relationship of collaboration, based on a long-term contract. The right to exclusivity applies to both parties: the entrepreneur cannot use more than one agent for the same area in the same branch of activity, and the agent cannot work for more than one enterprise in the same area, in the same branch of activity (Article 1743). The agent procures and presents the principal with orders from clients. It is then the principal who concludes the contracts, unless he/she has expressly attributed the agent powers of representation (Article 1752). The agent also, as a mediator, is compensated through commissions, which he/she collects only for deals that have a regular execution (Article 1748). Commercial agents must enrol in a special public register: failure to enrol results in nullity of the agency contract.

139. Finally, attention should be given to commission contracts, which are contracts that consist in an order to sell or buy on behalf of a dealer and in the name of a commission agent (Article 1731). Commission contracts are quite different from the other contracts illustrated in this chapter: here the commission agent has orders to buy or sell, but does so in his/her own name and not as a representative of the party he/she acts on behalf of.

Commission agents are compensated by the buyer through a commission corresponding to a certain percentage of the value of the deal. Thus, if the deal is not concluded the agent is not paid.

III. Insurance Contracts

140. Insurance contracts have the purpose of transferring some risks from individuals (so-called insured) to insurance companies: according to the definition provided in Article 1882, the insurer accepts to recover damages to assets the insured has suffered in the case of an adverse event, against the payment of a premium (indemnity insurance); or the insurer undertakes to pay a sum of money upon the occurrence of an event pertaining to human life (life insurance), either in periodic payments, such as the payment of an annuity, or in a single payment.

The regulation concerning the insurance sector is now contained in the Legislative Decree No. 209/2005 ('Consolidated Law on Insurance').

The reason for the insurance contract lies, therefore, in the transfer of the risk of the insured to the insurer through payment of a premium: as a consequence, if a risk never existed or ceased to exist before conclusion of the contract, the contract is null and the premium paid must be returned. If on the other hand, the risk ceases to exist after the conclusion of the contract, the latter is solved and the premium must be paid up to the time the solution is communicated to the insurer.

During the life of a contract the risk can increase or decrease: in both cases the insurer can withdraw from the insurance contract or, else, he/she can reduce or increase the premium accordingly.

The balance between the respective obligations of the contract can be modified from the beginning if the insured retains information or makes inexact declarations leading the insurer to be deceived as to the true nature of the assumed risk. In such a case, if the insured acted in bad faith or with negligence, the insurer may request the annulment of the contract; if however the insured acted without bad faith or negligence, the insurer may withdraw from the contract and, for damages which may have occurred before the discovery of the actual situation, the insured is paid an indemnity which is less than that provided by the contract and correspondent to the true situation.

According to Article 1900, the risks constituting the cause of the contract are those to which the assets or life of the insured is exposed by fortuity, force majeure, acts committed in bad faith by third parties, or facts caused by minor negligence on the part of the insured himself/herself. Unless otherwise stipulated however, cases of force majeure do not include earthquakes, wars, insurrections and situations of popular turmoil (Article 1912). Also, while risks due to the minor negligence of the insured are covered, those resulting from the bad faith or grave negligence of the insured are not indemnified, unless otherwise agreed.

The fact that the insured is the one exposed to the risk contemplated in the contract does not necessarily mean he/she is the party contracting the insurance: insurance can be contracted on others for whom there exists a legal or substantial economic interest (e.g., 'key man' insurance), and in this case, the insured party is different from the contracting party.

While in insurance contracts relating to individuals of economic interest, the name of such individuals is indicated to the contracting party, whereas in insurance contracts 'on behalf of those whom it may concern', the insured is whoever is exposed to the insured risk at the time of the damage and is not named in the contract.

The beneficiary of the insurance can also be a person different from the insured: this is so in the case of life insurance in favour of a third party, designated in the contract or with a subsequent declaration, who acquires a personal right with regard to the insurance firm (Article 1920).

Finally, there are forms of insurance having a legal rather than contractual source. These include mandatory liability insurance for motorists imposed by Law No. 990 of 1969 and the various forms of obligatory social insurance such as insurance against accidents on the job and professional illnesses.

IV. Bank Contracts

141. The two characteristic functions of banks are the collection of savings through mass deposits (passive function) and financing (active function). Two types of bank contracts correspond to this dual function: the collection of savings occurs through the contract of bank deposit, while financing is carried out, apart from the ordinary contract for a loan, through specific contracts for the opening of bank credit and for a bank advance.

Bank contracts are standard contracts which are concluded through the subscription by the client of general contract conditions offered by the bank. The general conditions of each bank conform to the Uniform Banking Laws, which the banks form together through the International Chambers of Commerce, banking contracts are, therefore, uniform for all users of banking services.

142. Through a bank deposit, clients give the bank a sum of money, which the bank takes into possession but is obliged to return to the client in the same currency (Article 1834) at some future time. This type of contract has two functions: in the interest of the client, it safeguards savings and, in the interest of the bank, it functions as credit, since from the pool of deposits made by its clients, the bank obtains money that it uses for financing activities. The provisions regarding loans (Article 1782, paragraph 2), as far as compatible, are applicable to bank deposits. In particular, among these, Article 1815, which provides that the bank must pay the client interests on the sums that he/she deposits.

Bank deposits are, as all bank contracts, current account contracts (Article 1852 and subsequent articles). Such contracts have a continuous performance: during their life deposits and withdrawals can be carried out and are annotated on the account without the need to sign a new contract for each deposit and withdrawal. The depositor can make multiple successive partial withdrawals under the same contract.

The bank deposit can be annotated on a special booklet for savings deposits issued by the bank and kept by the client, on which the bank records each deposit and withdrawal as it is carried out.

143. The opening of credit is the most common type of active banking contract. Through this contract, the bank undertakes to keep a certain sum of money at the disposition of the client for a given or undetermined period of time (Article 1842). This contract differs from a loan, which is widely used by banks for financing, in two ways: in contrast to a loan, a credit opening is a contract which is considered to be concluded at the very moment of the agreement, independently from the consignment of money; moreover, in a credit opening the bank obligates itself as debtor to the client for the accredited sum, and the client acquires, with regard to the bank, the right to use the consented credit (referred to as the store) in whole or in part. If the client uses part or all of the store, he/she comes under obligation to repay the sum withdrawn with the relative interests established in the contract.

Credit openings are normally in the form of a current account for which the client, during the time and up to the amount established in the contract, can make any number of withdrawals and can, with subsequent deposits, replenish the account.

Credit openings can be in the red (bank overdrafts) meaning without real or personal guarantees in favour of the bank, or guaranteed by mortgages, liens, performance guarantees, etc.

144. A subcategory of guaranteed credit openings are bank advances (Article 1846), characterized by the fact that the guarantee offered to the bank is constituted by liens on titles or goods.

Banks are furthermore used to granting advances on credits, or giving loans or credit openings guaranteed by liens on credits (Articles 2800 et seq.).

Finally, the interposition of the bank in the circulation of money is realized, from the active point of view, even though contracts which accomplish the function of credit do so only in a broad sense. It is the case of bank discounts, which is different from the advances on credits in that the credit of the client is not pledged to the bank, but sold to it for a sum, the sale price, less than the nominal amount of the credit. Discounts represent, in fact, the difference between the nominal amount of the credit and the lower price paid by the bank. Article 1858 defines the discount as a contract for which the client gives the bank a credit toward third parties that has not yet expired and the bank advances him the amount of the credit, upon deduction of a sum equal to the amount of the interest (the discount rate practiced by the bank) which will mature between the time of the advance and the expiration of the credit.

Bank discounts frequently have as their object credits resulting from bills of exchange or bank checks.

The bank can in turn use discounted credit with another bank, thus carrying out a re-discount.

V. Transport and Shipping

145. Transport contracts have as their object the execution of a particular service in favour of a customer: the service is the transportation of persons or objects from one place to another; the customer is the traveller in the transport of people, and the sender in the transport of objects. Those who undertake to perform the transport service are carriers (Article 1678). Carriers undertake to transport people or objects unharmed and intact to the agreed-upon destination. Carriers are, therefore, in default and responsible for damages both for failed completion of transport (or delays), as well as for damages that transported people may have suffered, or loss or damage to objects during transportation. Proof releasing the carrier from responsibility is different according to whether the transport is of objects or people.

According to Article 1693, in the transport of objects the carrier is responsible for the loss or damage of the things consigned to him for transport from the time he/she receives them until the time they are consigned to the addressee, unless he/she proves that loss or damage occurred from a case of fortuity, from defects in the transported object itself or, in any case, by fault of the sender.

In the transport of people Article 1681 provides a more rigorous rule: the carrier is released from responsibility only if he/she proves that he/she used every measure suitable to avoiding the damage.

Travellers, therefore, need only to prove the existence of the transport contract and the damage sustained, while the carrier has the burden of proving the inevitability of the damage on its part and, therefore, the lack of a cause-effect relationship between his/her activity of transportation and the damage sustained by the traveller. Furthermore, while in the transport of objects the responsibility can be mitigated through the contractual provision of presumptions of fortuity (Article 1694), in the transport of people, clauses limiting the responsibility of the carrier are not admitted (Article 1681).

146. Shipping is an order, on behalf of others but in one's own name, to carry out a transport contract and complete the accessory operations, such as customs clearance (Article 1737). Shipping agents are usually not responsible toward the sender for failure to perform the transport contract; and if they are consigned goods, their service and responsibility end when they in turn consign the goods to the carrier, unless they have also undertaken to transport them, in which case the provisions relative to the different figure of the shipping agent-carrier provided by Article 1741 apply.

VI. Other Contracts: Factoring and Leasing

147. Factoring is an atypical contract, introduced in Italy several years ago, whose object is to relieve producers and retailers from specific risk arising due to their customers' insolvency. Factors are entrepreneurs (normally companies) which interpose between the supplier of goods or services and his/her clients, stipulating with the supplier a contract whereby: (a) the supplier undertakes to submit to the factor contracts that are concluded or are to be concluded with the customer, and the factor reserves the right to approve the credits originating from such contracts, after having evaluated the solvability of the customers; (b) the supplier also undertakes to assign the factor his/her own credits which the factor has approved, and the factor, in turn, undertakes to pay the supplier, upon expiration of the credits, the agreed-upon sale price of the assignment (or the amount of the credits minus a sum covering the risks assumed and the costs of collection). This contract, therefore, does not constitute a financing operation, because the factor does not advance the amount of the credit, but rather a type of insurance of the credit, the factor's function being that of relieving the supplier of the risk relative to the insolvency of his/her clients.

Italy has not provided a complete regulation of factoring contracts. Few specific aspects are regulated, but a definition of this contract has not been provided as well as its structural and functional profiles have not been identified. Article 1 of Law No. 52 of 21 February 1991 sets the conditions which are necessary for the applicability of the new discipline, explicitly indicating that in their absence the provisions of the Civil Code on credit assignments will apply: (a) the assignor must be an entrepreneur; (b) the credits assigned must originate from contracts stipulated by the assignor in the operation of the enterprise; (c) the assignee must be a company or legal entity, provided that its company's purpose includes the purchase of credits originating in the operation of an enterprise, and the company's capital or the endowment fund of the same must not be less than ten times as much as the minimum capital required for a joint-stock company.

The Bank of Italy keeps the register of the companies exercising a factoring activity and supervises their conduct.

148. Another atypical contract which has been widely used in Italy for some time, based on the American model, is the leasing contract, which is regulated by the Law Decree No. 124 of 4 August 2017, paragraphs 136 et seq. Here also there is a peculiar figure of enterprise – the leasing enterprise – which interposes between two entrepreneurs: on one side, the producing or distributing entrepreneurs of industrial installations or high technology machinery; on the other, the entrepreneurs using such productive instruments in their businesses.

Leasing contracts are contracts between the leasing enterprise and the user, whereby: (a) the leasing enterprise undertakes to allow the user the use of the item for a certain period of time, usually less than the presumed duration of the item's economic life; in favour of the user, it can be agreed that, at the end of the contract's term, he/she will have the option to extend the term of the contract or to purchase the item; (b) in turn, the user assumes the risks related to the leased item, such as damage, destruction or deterioration, and undertakes to pay a periodic fee to the leasing enterprise, the total of which tends, in relation to the duration of the contract, to equal the capital value of the item, plus the interests and the risk and profit of the leasing enterprise; furthermore a fee can be set out, lower than the one previously agreed upon, for contracts including the possibility to extend the lease, or an additional price for contracts providing an option to buy at the expiration of the lease.

This contract accomplishes a function of financing, as it is equivalent to a loan made by the leasing enterprise to the user, but is more advantageous for the leasing enterprise or contrarily for the user depending on what actually turns out to be the role played by the risk of obsolescence of the item. If the item becomes obsolete after the expiration of the contract, the greatest advantage is enjoyed by the leasing enterprise, which can lease to a new user, with the payment of new fees, an item whose entire value has been earned or, if the original user exercises the pre-agreed right to extend the contract or purchase the item, further fees or the agreed-upon purchase price are obtained on top of the already realized profit.

If, however, the item becomes obsolete in correspondence with the expiration of the contract, the user will have received the greatest advantage, given that he/she may return the item at the moment it has become economically valueless.

Part II. Economic System and Enterprises

Chapter 1. State Intervention in Economic Activities

149. In the Italian 'economic constitution' ample space is dedicated to the intervention of public powers in the economy.

State intervention in economy represents a fundamental duty of the Public Administration directed at increasing the collective economic well-being of the nation. The Italian system, in particular, guarantees the principles of private property (even though there are limitations in view of the social function for which it is destined: Article 42 of the Constitution) and freedom of economic initiative (although that initiative must be directed and coordinated for social purposes: Article 41 of the Constitution).

State interventions in the economy can assume diverse and complex forms, such as the direct exercise of economic activities through public economic entities and autonomous enterprises; the direction and control on the part of the Public Administration of private and semi-public enterprises (i.e., private enterprises, whose stock capital is totally or partly State held).

In the last twenty years Italy has undertaken a wide privatization process. The majority of privatization proceeds have been raised through public offering of shares on the stock market. This feature has deeply changed the ways through which the State intervenes in economic activities.

150. In relation to the ever-growing State intervention in economic activities, numerous bodies and ministries regulate economic activities: CNEL (the National Committee on the Economy and Work), a constitutional body (Article 99 of the Constitution) with the auxiliary functions of the Chamber and Senate and the government, and representing the category of subjects who concur in national production (it is composed of the president and by 111 members chosen from experts and representatives of the productive categories); the Ministry of Economy and Finance; the Ministry of Economic Development.

Also local authorities (regions, etc.) are entitled to intervene in specific areas of the economy; besides concurring with the State in economic planning, they determine local development programs in harmony with national planning.

From the time of the formal recognition of the regions, the majority of administrative functions, above all in agriculture, industry and commerce have, in fact, been transferred to these territorial bodies, whereas the State continues, besides the duties of coordination, to carry out the powers inherent to international and community relations.

151. Among the various forms of public intervention in the economy, particular importance is assumed by the system of State holdings: this system consists of the ownership of stocks in private joint-stock companies by a public entity, called a 'management body', controlled by the State.

The system of State holdings dates back to the end of the nineteenth century: already at that time some laws provided for the possibility of the State to purchase stock in joint-stock companies, and also local territorial bodies took advantage of that possibility to construct their own management bodies, such as municipal enterprises for aqueducts and electric energy.

After the end of World War I, the State intervened to save metallurgic, iron and steel industries from economic crisis; in 1929, following the worldwide economic crisis, the State intervened in order to save banks and created two management bodies: IRI (the Institute for Industrial Reconstruction) and IMI (the Italian Movables Institute), which acquired the stocks held by the banks. In 1953, ENI (the National Body on Hydrocarbons) was created, grouping the various companies with public shareholdings previously operating in the field of hydrocarbons (Azienda Generale Italiana Petroli (AGIP), Azienda Nazionale Idrogenazione Combustibili (ANIC), Società Nazionale Metanodotti (SNAM), etc.)

Joint-stock companies are considered to be in public hands if the State or some other public entity holds the majority or at least a parcel of shares, guaranteeing the control of the company; such companies, however, do not acquire the status of public entity, but continue to be private, even though Articles 2449–2451 of the Civil Code provide a different set of provisions whenever there is a public shareholder or the company is of national interest, since they authorize the public shareholder to assume a position of command with different instruments other than ordinary laws. The system has changed considerably since 1992, when the Italian privatization programme was started (Law 359/1992). IRI was converted, along with the other three main State holdings, National Corporation of Electrical Energy (ENEL) (electricity), ENI (petrochemical), INA (insurance), into public limited companies, with the government as the sole shareholder. This was done to create the conditions 'to go public' and to make such companies subject to the provisions of civil law.

IRI had a mandate to privatize the assets under its ownership, and pursued a policy of active management and strategic repositioning as a means of maximizing the value of its assets. Between 1992 and its closure in June of 2000, over 30% of the proceeds raised by the Italian privatization program were generated from the sale of assets held by IRI.

152. One of the tools that the Italian Government used to continue controlling enterprises after the privatization process were golden shares. Golden shares provide governments with special powers and veto rights in partially privatized companies, and have generally served governments as a mean to protect privatized companies from hostile takeovers on public policy grounds.

In Italy, golden shares were initially broadly defined. The Italian law of 1994 provided the State with special powers that could be used to safeguard its vital interests, in particular public order, safety, health and defence. However, this circumstance created several concerns with respect to their effect on free movement of capital and establishment. Therefore, in order to meet the concerns expressed by the EU, through the adoption of Law 488/1999 the Italian Government revised its golden share rules to clarify their scope and use them for very limited public interest reasons.

The new law required that both the introduction and the exercise of golden share powers had to be founded on overriding requirements of the general interest and be proportionate to the objective being pursued, in compliance with the fundamental principles of the Community law, including the non-discrimination criteria.

Notwithstanding the changes in the law, the European Court of Justice ruled in 2009 that the special powers recognized to the Italian Government by the law of 1999 were still in contrast with the provision of the EU Treaty aimed at fostering the free movement of capitals within the internal market.

153. As pointed out in paragraph 56 the CIPE is a governmental body chaired by the president of the Council of Ministers and made up of thirteen permanent members (the Minister for the Economy and Finance, the Minister for Foreign Affairs, the Minister for Economic Development, the Minister for Infrastructure and Transport, the Minister for Labour and Social Policies, the Minister for Agricultural and Forestry Policies, the Minister for the Environment and the Protection of the Soil and Sea, the Minister for Cultural Goods and Activities, the Minister for Education, Universities and Research, the Minister for European Policies, the Minister for Relations with the Regions, the Minister for Tourism, the Chairman of the Conference of the Presidents of the Autonomous Regions and Provinces).

CIPE, which was set up in 1967, has a coordination function in the planning of the economic policy. It examines the general socio-economic situation with a view to the adoption of cyclical measures; identifies the initiatives which are necessary in order to achieve the objectives of economic policy; allocates financial resources to development programs; approves the public investment plans.

The main issues CIPE examines concern the Public Finance Decision, the Forecasting and Planning Report and the National Statistical Program; the Strategic Infrastructure Program of the Objective Law (Law 443/2001); the investment plans and conventions of the main public concessionaires (Rete Femoviana Italiana (RFI), Ente Nationale Aviatione Civile (ENAC), Azienda Nationale Autonoma delle Strade (ANAS), Ente Nationale di Assistenza al Volo (ENAV)), and leading private concessionaires for motorways, airports, railways, water and ports; changes in the charges of the above-mentioned concessionaires and public-private partnerships examined by the PPP Task Force; the distribution of the financial resources of the Development and Cohesion Fund (FSC) and of the funds to which it supplies resources that operate in the following fields: labour mobility, social policies, support for firms, research, technological innovation, the environment, security, and education; the National Research Programme, the National Plan for the Reduction of the Emissions of the

Gases responsible for the Greenhouse Effect, the School Buildings Safety Programme, the Road Safety Programme, the Three-Year Public Works Programmes of individual government departments, the Housing Plan; the instruments for the support of firms; the distribution of the financial resources of the National Health Fund; the activation of the Public Investment Monitoring (MIP) system and the complete implementation of the Individual Project Code (CUP).

To determine the goals of the national economic policy, the State holds competitions within the regions; programmes for development within a province must be harmonized with the national policy and are determined by regions through competition of local territorial entities, according to the modalities provided by the statutes of that province.

It should in any case be pointed out that the experience of a unified national policy for the whole of Italy, pushed ahead in the late sixties, has not been followed up: it was exercised only in certain fields and often only episodically through laws that seldom tended to meet contingencies.

Chapter 2. Subsidies, Contributions and Fiscal Discounts

154. In order to incentivize particular economic activities, different forms of subsidies, sunk contributions, premiums, direct and indirect financing – especially in the form of loans facilitated by the payment of reduced interest and long-term rates – and other facilitations, such as exemption from or reduction of taxes on goods manufactured and services offered, have been provided.

With regard to these types of intervention, usually provided for in programmatic laws, it must be noted that, while generally speaking no right exists on the part of applicants to necessarily receive the above-mentioned aid, for the exemptions and fiscal reductions conceded by the law an actual right does exist. Such forms of aid and incentive are provided for in the fields of agriculture, fishing, industry, handicrafts and commerce.

155. In agriculture, it is worth noticing that the interventions carried out by AGEA (the Agency for Disbursements in the Agriculture) in support of the sale of different products pursuant to the enactment of the Regulations of the EU. The Agency is entitled to coordinate the application of EC Rules recognizing aids in the agricultural fields. The Agency also coordinates the activity of the payers.

156. The forms of economic aid from the State in favour of industry have always been considerable. The law provides for several forms of aid in favour of particular fields of industry, such as the ship-building, textile, manufacturing, iron and steel, publishing and newspaper and aeronautical industries, etc.

The adoption of Law No. 662/1996 has created new forms of aid to industries aimed at fostering local development through negotiating instruments. The negotiated planning tool is an important device for the implementation of local development policies. Such procedure envisages the involvement of both public and private players in order to improve the development of the local territory.

An essential aspect of such aids is the 'negotiation' for the drafting of an agreement among all the parties involved (central administrations, local administrations, private enterprises, trade unions, etc.). Parties negotiate for the concession of financial incentives to enterprises and the creation of favourable conditions (social, economic and in terms of infrastructures) to establish productive facilities and to create new jobs.

There are several instruments allowing for 'negotiated planning', each of them is different in terms of finality, procedures and parties involved.

The Planning Contract (Contratto di programma), is an aid suitable for groups and multinationals. It consists of signing of a 'contract' – between the local administration and the enterprise or group of enterprises – whose aim is to gain access to various forms of incentives, thus stimulating the creation of a manufacturing plant that would have a significant economic impact on the local territory in terms of jobs. The Territorial Pact (Patto territoriale) is based on an agreement, between a number of parties (enterprises, local authorities, industrial and labour associations, etc.), for the implementation of an economic stimulus project characterized by specific objectives for the development of the local economy. The Pact provides for incentives for enterprises and other actions ranging from the construction of infrastructures to the implementation of more flexible conditions in the management of administration and labour.

The Area Contract (Contratto d'area) is an economic tool especially created for low growth and employment areas. It is based on an agreement between trade unions and employer's associations to ensure more flexible labour conditions and on the availability of logistic structures that are in a position to attract new investments. The Area Contract is also based on the commitment of public local administrations to streamline the procedures relating to the authorization for the setting up of new businesses and the construction of the required infrastructure.

157. A Fund of Guarantees for SMEs is provided by the Ministry of Economic Development in order to foster SMEs' access to credit. The Fund intervenes whenever an SME applies for bank credit, by providing a State guarantee.

158. The forms of fiscal incentives available are various and include direct contributions, tax breaks, low-interest funding, government guarantees for credit, etc. Incentives are financed by European, national and/or regional funds. As a general rule, there is a relationship between the size of the incentive and the development level of the 'disadvantaged' areas, where the incentive is applicable. Regional areas facing lower levels of development can rely on higher incentives (e.g., for new investments, R&D activities, for exports and international business).

Some incentives are granted automatically, thus without a formal application or a preliminary authorization from the competent authority. Other incentives and bonuses are granted in some sectors, according to specific rules.

Chapter 3. Freedom of Competition

§1. General Principles and Repression of Unfair Competition

159. Already in the Civil Code of 1942, rules were provided on the presumption of an economic system in which, normally, commercial entrepreneurs operate in a situation of free competition. This basic choice was substantially confirmed in the Constitution of 1948, where Article 41 provides for freedom of private economic initiative. This statutory choice adheres to the wide-spread opinion that this system of competition constitutes the best instrument for carrying out economic development: it is presumed that entrepreneurs are thus induced to improve the quality of their products or services without being able to arbitrarily raise their prices, in order to prevail over competitors. It follows, therefore, that in the Italian system, entrepreneurs are usually unable to legally obtain monopoly positions, whereas the protection of the ability to earn is guaranteed, in the sense that the same entrepreneurs are attributed the right to try to realize a profit through the operation of a competitive activity.

The means by which competition is exercised must, however, correspond to professional ethics, in the sense that no entrepreneur can use unfair methods of competition. Faced with acts of unfair competition, any entrepreneur may take judicial action against an unfair competitor.

160. In the Civil Code the prohibition of unfair competition is set out in Article 2598, which, along with the provisions that repress the usurpation of absolute rights on distinctive signs and on inventions remaining intact, also prohibits:

(a) acts causing confusion (i.e., slavish imitation of the products of a competitor or any other act likely to create confusion with the products or the activity of another competitor);
(b) acts of denigration, which consist in the spreading of information or opinions on the products or the activity of a competitor likely to discredit him; (c) acts of boasting, that consist of the appropriation of the qualities of the products or the activities of a competitor; (d) any other act that does not conform to the principles of professional correctness, or which is likely to damage another competitor.

A sentence ascertaining an act of unfair competition prohibits its continuation and orders the appropriate action to eliminate its consequences. If the act was carried out wilfully or with negligence (negligence being presumed), the guilty party is sentenced to damages, and the publication of the sentence can be ordered.

§2. Conventional Limitations on Competition: Cartels and Consortiums

161. Conventional limitations can be imposed on competition. These are limitations established in special trade agreements which, for the most part, are unfavourably judged by the legislature, their importance thus tending to be narrowed. Consequently the validity of an autonomous agreement of non-competition is recognized, but only if it can be proved that it was stipulated in a written instrument. It is limited to a certain area and a certain activity, and it has a duration of not more than five years (if it exceeds five years, the duration of the obligation to abstain from competition is automatically reduced to five years: Article 2596, Article 2125 and Article 2557 paragraph 3).

162. The limitations imposed by the provisions of Article 2596 also apply to other restrictive practices on competition, such as cartels, which are multilateral contracts with which two or more competing entrepreneurs establish reciprocal restrictions on their activities: for example, they undertake not to sell their products at a price lower than that fixed in the contract, or they divide the territory of distribution of the products into different areas, or they establish the total quantity of merchandise to be produced by all the enterprises together and then the production share of each individual enterprise.

163. Another restrictive practice on competition, which, however, is not contained in the terms of Article 2596, is constituted by consortiums for the coordination of production and trade. These are defined by Article 2602 as contracts by which two or more entrepreneurs establish a common organization to regulate and carry out certain steps of the respective enterprises. They differ in respect to cartels in that they originate a common organization, the duty of which is to coordinate the economic activity of the individual entrepreneurs of the consortium and to supervise their exact compliance with the responsibilities undertaken with the consortium contract. Originally, like cartels, consortiums were only an oligopolistic practice, but later the consortium contract proved to be an instrument capable of reinforcing one's position on the market especially in cases of medium and small enterprises, and, therefore, effective in performing an anti-monopolistic function. As a consequence, the legislative attitude with regard to this type of contract changed: the original provisions of the Civil Code, inspired by restriction, were amended by Law No. 377 of 1976 with provisions in favour of consortiums.

§3. Legal Limitations on Competition: Monopolies and Antitrust Legislation

164. Along with freedom of competition, the same legislature has imposed limitations on competition. These are of two types. First, there are legal prohibitions on competition enforced with those who transfer a business (Article 2557), employees in regard to the entrepreneur employing them (Article 2105), partners in general partnerships and limited partnerships (Articles 2301 and 2315), and directors of joint-stock companies (Articles 2390, 2465, 2487). This involves a series of prohibitions which the legislature has considered necessary for the execution in good faith of the different relationships taken into consideration, even when the contracting parties have not contemplated any specific provisions.

165. Another set of legal limitations demonstrates that the legislature acknowledges the fact that the system of freedom of competition is not the best one to satisfy general interests. In this perspective, the Code of 1942 has already established that competition must be conducted in such a way so as to not prejudice national economic interests (Article 2595); similarly the wording of the Constitution (Article 41, paragraph 2), for the purposes of general utility, permits the law to 'reserve from the beginning or subsequently transfer, by means of expropriation and save for an indemnity, to the State, to public entities or to pools of workers or users, certain enterprises or categories of enterprises, which relate to essential public services, to energy sources or to situations of monopoly, and which are characterized by being of general pre-eminent interest' (Article 43).

In cases of enterprises operated in conditions of legal monopoly, the Code obligates the monopolist to negotiate with anyone requesting the services that are the object of the enterprise's activity with equality of treatment (Article 2597).

166. Apart from these few provisions, the Italian system used to lack antitrust legislation to prevent the formation of monopolies, to repress the abuse of monopolistic positions and to regulate the phenomenon of agreements between enterprises in restraint of trade. The provisions of the Civil Code deal exclusively with the fact that the overly broad limits to competition conventionally assumed can prejudice the freedom of the entrepreneur who accepted them, whereas no discipline exists to protect competition as a factor which regulates the economic course.

Enterprises have in fact always demonstrated the tendency of creating agreements and connections directed at the accomplishment of reciprocal advantages, and the carrying out of enterprise combinations and integrations can be accomplished through various economic and legal figures: acquisitions of enterprises, mergers, combinations under the same economic party, and joint-ventures. Though it is evident that the antitrust law does not have as its objective barring the natural growth of the enterprise, it is, however, necessary to create a set of provisions directed at preventing agreements between competing enterprises, dominating positions and monopolies on the market on the part of individual enterprises that allow such enterprises to unilaterally determine their market policies (especially in matters of prices), without being subjected to restraints resulting from the existence of competition on the part of other enterprises.

Repression of the abuse of monopolistic positions was possible in Italy only with the provisions of the Treaty of the European Economic Community, which contains anti-monopolistic legislation partially modelled after the American example. Article 81 (now Article 101) of the Treaty prohibits, in fact, agreements which have as their purpose the limiting of competition. However, this article refers only to those abuses that can be detrimental to the commerce between Member States of the Community, and does not deal with national or provincial agreements, the effects of which are produced only within one of the Member States without important repercussions on intra-community commercial trade. Article 82 (now Article 102) of the Treaty declares the abusive exploitation by one or more enterprise of a dominant position on the common market or substantial part of the common market incompatible with the community market and so prohibits it: however, this legal provision proved to be a weak instrument in the control of enterprise combinations, mainly because it can be used only when one of the enterprises participating in the operation already holds a dominant position prior to the combination.

167. With Law No. 287 of 10 October 1990, finally, also in Italy, a set of law provisions was introduced directed at protecting competition and trade. For that purpose the *Autorità Garante della concorrenza e del Mercato* (AGCM) was established. Its headquarters are in Rome, and it is composed of a President and four members. The Authority has informative and consultative powers, as well as the power to conduct investigations of general nature when certain circumstances lead to the presumption that competition is being prevented, restricted or falsified, or to impose sanctions and inhibit illicit behaviours.

168. The Italian antitrust law applies to agreements, abuses of dominant positions and mergers among enterprises (of which a precise definition is given) that do not already fall in the scope of application of Community law. The provisions apply to private enterprises, public enterprises and enterprises with a prevalence of State shareholdings; they do not apply, on the other hand, to enterprises which, by legal provision, exercise the management of services of general economic interest or which operate on the market as monopolies, for everything closely connected to the accomplishment of the specific duties entrusted to them.

Law No. 52/1996 has empowered the National Authority to apply the competition rules contained in the Treaty of Rome. With the entry into force of the EC Regulation No. 1/2003, which lays down a new set of procedural rules and allows for a wider involvement of National Competition Authorities in the enforcement of EC law, the Authority is now competent to apply community law to practices that are taking place in the national geographic market or within a substantial part of it and which are affecting trade between Member States.

169. Agreements which are prohibited and considered null are those which prevent, restrict or alter in a significant manner competition on the national market or a considerable part of it. Examples of activities which can be prohibited are: (a) directly or indirectly fixing purchase or selling prices or other contractual conditions; (b) preventing or limiting production, outlets or access to the market, investments, technical and technological development; (c) dividing the market or the sources of supply; (d) applying contractual conditions that are objectively different for equivalent goods or services in commercial relationships with other contracting parties; (e) and subordinating the conclusion of contracts to the undertaking on the part of the other contracting parties to provide supplementary services which, by their nature or according to commercial customs, do not relate in any way to the object of the captioned contract. Derogations, however, are provided and must be permitted when enterprises can make improvements on the conditions under which goods are offered to consumers on the market which would create a substantial benefit for consumers.

In 2001, powers of the Authority have been extended to claims related to the abuse of 'economic dependence', for example, refusal to deal, burdensome or discriminatory contract conditions, etc. The Authority may fine enterprises for the abuse of economic dependence where their conduct 'is relevant to the protection of competition and the free market'.

170. A concentration between undertakings is: (a) a merger of two or more previously independent undertakings; (b) the acquisition of control; (c) the creation of a joint-venture mergers is prohibited when they create or strengthen a dominant position.

171. If the Authority finds out an infringement due to agreements or abuses of a dominant position, it fixes a deadline for their elimination. In cases of serious violations, it also orders the application of a pecuniary administrative sanction of no more than 10%, of the turnover realized by the enterprise in its previous operation. If the merger is restrictive, the Authority prohibits its performance; if it has already been carried out, it can order the measures necessary to renew conditions of actual competition and eliminate the distorting effects. In the event of infringement of the prohibition, the Authority applies pecuniary administrative sanctions in the same measure of those provided for violations in cases of agreements and abuses of dominant positions.

172. It should finally be noted that with the above-mentioned law, the concept of control over of an enterprise, contained in Article 2359 of the Civil Code, was also redefined within the limits of the discipline on merger operations. Therefore, in this regard, there is control, in addition to the cases contemplated in Article 2359 of the Civil Code, also in cases regarding rights, contracts and other legal relationships which confer, by themselves or jointly, the possibility of exercising a determinant influence on the activities of an enterprise, also by means of: (a) rights on the whole or part of the assets of an enterprise; (b) rights, contracts or other legal relationships which confer a determinant influence on the composition, resolutions or decisions of the bodies of the enterprise.

173. Finally, the Legislative Decree No. 3 adopted on 19 January 2017 pursuant to Directive 2014/04/EU, now regulates the compensation for violation of antitrust law, with the aim of: (i) uniforming the legislation concerning antitrust compensation in different Member States; and (ii) strengthening the protection accorded to any subject which suffered an antitrust damage. In addition, mandatory competence is established in favour of the specialized sections in Milan, Rome and Naples in issues related to antitrust provisions.

Chapter 4. State Regulation of the Contractual Provisions for Entrepreneurial Activities

§1. Consumer Protection

I. General Principles

174. The classification of consumer rights is quite detailed, but it can be summarized as follows: consumers have the right to be informed and warned, to be heard, to be represented and to be indemnified. These rights, which correspond in a large part to those contained in the Community Resolution of 1975 regarding a preliminary programme for a policy of consumer protection and information, have been finally stated in the Consumer Code, which was approved on 23 October 2005.

The Code summarizes and reorganizes all the rules and provisions related to consumer law. Specifically, Article 2 of Consumer Code sets the fundamental rights of consumers and users to protection of health, to safety and quality of products and services, to adequate information and correct advertising, to education for consumers, to honesty, transparency and equity in contractual relationships, to the promotion and the development of free, voluntary and democratic consumers associations, to the provision of public utilities that respect quality and efficiency standards.

II. Information for Consumer Protection

175. Commercial advertising is the most important means of information to consumers. For this reason, the ways and forms of presenting advertisements, their global volume, and their persuasive effect require regulation in order to assure that they do not cross the line from instrument of information to instrument of persuasion by utilizing ways and forms that conflict with the need to protect consumers. The Italian experience, due to initial gaps in legislation, evolved according to some specific guidelines. First, supervision of advertising was carried out on individual advertisements rather than on the advertising activity as a whole. Consequently judgments on the opportunity, legitimacy and fairness of advertisements were always limited to the individual, contingent advertisement, and the global perspective on which supervision should be based was sacrificed. Furthermore, based on the supposition that advertising was informative, supervision was almost always carried out with a view to verifying that the advertisement corresponded to the real characteristics of the product.

From here, legislation and jurisprudence developed in order to repress deceptive advertising (aimed at misleading consumers); this was applicable to only a small portion of advertisements because supervision was organized with instruments that were not suitable since they mostly aimed at repressing acts of unfair competition among entrepreneurs, rather than protecting consumers. In fact with the use of legal provisions on unfair competition, in particular of Article 2598 of the Civil Code, the interests directly protected were those of the entrepreneurs, given that all the provisions were oriented to assuring economic dealers freedom of competition on the market according to the criteria of professional correctness and fairness.

176. The situation changed when the Legislative Decree No. 74 of 25 January 1992, was approved in order to enact the EEC Directive No. 450 of 1984 for the approximation of the statutory, regulatory and administrative legal provisions of the Member States in matters of deceptive advertising.

The Directive aimed at preventing advertising which, 'in any way, including its presentation, misleads or is likely to mislead the people to whom it is directed or whom it reaches and which, given its deceptive character, could prejudice the economic behaviour of said people or which, for this reason, damages or could damage a competitor'.

The scope of the legislative intervention was, therefore, limited to advertisements which misled the public or created confusion among products and caused damage to competitors.

Regarding techniques of protection, consumer protection and the protection of competing entrepreneurs operated on the administrative level: the Competition Authority, instituted with the antitrust law, was authorized to decide on the petitions for inhibitory injunctions filed by competitors, consumers, associations and organizations, as well as public administrations.

Comparative advertising was also allowed and a specific legislation on this issue (Law No. 67/2000) provided that a comparative advertisement should not be misleading or unfair.

177. The said discipline was introduced into a system characterized by self-discipline of advertising matters. Until that moment, the lack of specific legislation disciplining advertising and the consequent absence of statuary controls had led to the creation of a role of substitution for the jury of self-discipline, which had operated with margins of autonomy and particular effectiveness. The prevalence of the self-disciplinary instrument with respect to the statutory regulation characterizes the contents of Article 8 of the Decree: this Article, which was directed at disciplining the relationship between the administrative and jurisdictional protection provided by the new discipline and the self-disciplinary control, provided that parties, to obtain an order inhibiting acts of deceptive advertising, could apply to 'autonomous and voluntary bodies of self-discipline'. The above-mentioned Article furthermore provided that once engaged in proceedings before the self-disciplinary body, the parties can abstain from instituting proceedings before the Competition Authority until the final decision of the self-disciplinary body was rendered. It also provided that in the event that a petition to the Authority was already filed, any interested party could request that the Authority suspend the proceedings while awaiting the decision of the self-disciplinary body.

178. Finally, in 2007, Italy implemented the EU Directive 2005/29/CE concerning unfair commercial practices in the European market, through the approval of two legislative decrees: Legislative Decree No. 145/2007 on misleading advertising for the protection of traders in their commercial relations and Legislative Decree No. 146/2007 on business-to-consumers unfair commercial practices. The two decrees replace the previous legislation, including that on deceptive and comparative advertising and consolidate it in the Consumer Code.

The new rules apply not only to advertising but also to any action, omission, declaration or commercial communication aimed at promoting or selling goods or services.

The objective is to sanction any behaviour that can alter the consumer's attitude to take an informed decision and lead him, through coercion or undue influence, to take a decision that in a normal situation he/she wouldn't have taken.

Misleading or aggressive practices are specifically listed. Briefly, according to Decree No. 146, it is forbidden: to conduct personal visits to the consumer's home ignoring the consumer's request to leave or not to return; to make persistent and unwanted solicitations by telephone, fax, e-mail or other remote media; to include in an advertisement a direct exhortation to children to buy advertised products or persuade their parents or other adults to buy advertised products for them, without prejudice to the provisions of Legislative Decree No. 177 of 31 July 2005 and subsequent amendments; create the false impression that the consumer has already won or will win a prize or other equivalent benefit, when in fact either there is no prize or other equivalent benefit, or taking any action in relation to claiming the prize or other equivalent benefit is subject to the consumer paying money or incurring a cost; to explicitly inform consumers that if they do not buy the product or service, the trader's job or livelihood will be in jeopardy; to describe a product as 'gratis', 'free', 'without charge' or similar if the consumer has to pay anything other than the unavoidable cost of responding to the commercial communication and collecting or paying for delivery of the item; to display a trust mark, quality mark or an equivalent without having obtained the necessary authorization; to create the impression that the consumer cannot leave the premises until a contract is executed; to give false information, including overall presentation, that deceives or is likely to deceive the average consumer, even if the information is factually correct, in relation to the existence or nature of the product, its properties, its price, etc. When these cases occur, the consumer doesn't need to prove that such behaviours are likely to distort his/her commercial choice.

The new rules have also strengthened sanctions and investigative powers of the Competition Authority.

179. It should finally be remembered that a very effective control in these matters is also carried out by criminal jurisprudence. It is, however, a control limited to the most serious violations in which it is possible to recognize the grounds of a crime. The provisions referred to are those which repress fraud in commerce (Article 515 of the Penal Code); the sale of substances that are not genuine (Article 516); the sale or trade of industrial products with names, marks or distinctive signs likely to deceive the purchaser on their origin, source or quality (Article 517); denigration by means of advertising (Article 595); confidence tricks (Article 640); and the abuse of popular credulity (Article 661). A different case is that of the contrast of the advertisement with the criminal provisions directed at the protection of family and public morals (Articles 565, 528, 725, 726 of the Penal Code). In any case it should be noted that the repressive sanction does not always turn out to be effective: in many cases the sanction can be extinguished by payment of a sum of money, and thus the violation, being payable, comes to be computed as a cost of advertising initiative.

180. From this standpoint, it seems preferable to entrust the supervision of advertising to the legislature. In some cases there exist true prohibitions on advertising activity: for example, the bar on advertising activity for smoker's products and alcoholic beverages (Law No. 165 of 10 April 1962 and Ministerial Decree No. 425 of 30 November 1991, containing the regulation concerning the enactment of Articles 13, 15 and 16 of the EEC Directive of 1989, relative to television advertisement of tobacco products and alcoholic drinks and to the protection of minors); the bar on advertising activity for unauthorized sales at unauthorized premiums (Article 124 of Law Decree No. 1933 of 19 October 1930). There are also administrative controls in some merchandising fields which are carried out through preventative censuring: as in the medicinal, mineral water, medical and surgical product fields (Royal Decree No. 1265 of 27 July 1934); dietetic products (Law No. 327 of 20 March 1951); and touristic and hotel advertising (Royal Decree No. 2523 of 23 November 1936; Royal Decree No. 2049 of 24 October 1935). Furthermore running deceptive advertisements regarding food and agricultural products is prohibited (Law No. 283 of 30 April 1962, and Law No. 441 of 26 February 1963), and a discipline regarding the labelling of products, for the moment limited to food products, has been introduced (Presidential Decree No. 322 of 18 March 1982, in enforcing EEC Directives 79/182 of 1978 and 94 of 1977). In conclusion it should be remembered that in Italy, a discipline of radio and television advertising has been introduced in 1990 (Article 8 of Law 223 of 1990).

III. Safety and Quality of Products

181. The sale guarantees that involve the indication of information to the purchaser are disciplined in the Civil Code, in particular by Articles 1490 et seq., under a perspective which considers only the hypothesis in which the product presents concealed defects or is lacking essential qualities. The presence of evident defects excludes, therefore, the protection of the consumer.

In the Italian Civil Code the seller is obliged to guarantee the buyer against concealed defects of the article (Article 1476 No. 3 of the Civil Code). This involves the material defects of the Article which the purchaser was not aware of at the time of the contract, or which he/she could not easily recognize (Articles 1490 paragraph 1 and 1491 of the Civil Code). The lack of qualities promised or of essential qualities of the object is considered comparable to a concealed defect (Article 1497). The purchaser, after having filed a timely complaint, has one year's time, from the consignment of the object, to enforce his/her guarantee in court and, in any case, has the right to compensation for damages sustained, unless the seller proves that he/she overlooked the defects without fault (Article 1494, paragraph 1).

Those provisions of the Italian Civil Code have a further limit: being structured on the basis of the individual sale's model of the seventeenth century tradition, they discipline the contractual relationship between the purchaser and the retailer, as well as the individual relationships which make up the chain of distribution of the products, but do not regard the relationship between productive enterprises and product purchasers. Furthermore, the control on the contents of the guarantee, which to be effective should occur beforehand at a legislative level, is practically delegated to the purchaser, through his/her possibility of instituting legal proceedings.

182. With the above-mentioned lack of statutory provisions, the implementation of the discipline dictated in matters of responsibility for damage derived from defective products by EEC Directive No. 374/1985 was very important. The Decree enforcing the Directive (Presidential Decree No. 224 of 24 May 1988) establishes that the manufacturer is responsible for damage caused by a defect of his/her product (Article 1) and sets out the general definition of defectiveness of a product as lack of safety which the public at large can legitimately expect to be present (Article 5 following the provision of Article 6 of the Directive). The whole discipline was transferred in 2005 in the Consumer Code (Articles 114 et seq.).

183. First, it should be noted that the correspondence of the defectiveness to the legitimate expectations of safety by the public consists of all the possible flaws and defects of manufacture, construction and information: once the absolute liability of the manufacturer has been affirmed, and once the definition of defectiveness has been based on the legitimate public expectations of safety, that tripartition is left with a merely descriptive role.

To determine the legitimacy of the expectations of safety, objective reference parameters are set out. These consist in a set of non-peremptory circumstances in light of which the general rule can be interpreted and applied. Those circumstances are: (a) the way in which the product was put into circulation, its presentation, its apparent characteristics, the instructions and warnings provided; (b) the use for which the product can reasonably be destined and consumers' behaviours which, in relation to it, can be reasonably foreseen; (c) the time in which the product was put into circulation (Article 117).

The circumstances mentioned in letter a) trace back to the informative activity of the producer. The more and better informed the user is on the correct use and characteristics of the product, the safer that product will be considered. The awareness thus imparted to the user, which permits safe use, not only constitutes the measure of the manufacture's duty of care, but a significant term of reference for evaluating the acceptability of the risk. Correct and complete information can in fact neutralize the intrinsic danger of some characteristics of the product at the moment of their actual use. The same function is accomplished by the availability of 'well-known' information, which is referred to by the other circumstance indicated in the provision, the existence of 'apparent characteristics'.

It should be noted that the reference to awareness (provided by the manufacturer or derived from the apparent characteristics) of the conditions of use, besides determining the degree of reasonability for the expectations of safety, it implicitly introduces, as an integrative criterion of evaluation of the danger of the product, that of the comparative evaluation between danger and benefit. Granted that it would obviously be unreasonable to expect absolute safety, the real degree of danger, and, therefore, of defectiveness, is determined also in relation to the actual capacity of the user to be aware of the risks connected to the use of the product, and to compare them with the expected benefits.

According to letter b) of Article 117, an expectation of safety referred to an unreasonable use of the product is not legitimate. It is the behaviour of the user that determines the limit of acceptability of the risk, from which an abnormal use of the product is in fact excluded. The rule undergoes, however, a correction in relation to intrinsically unreasonable uses which can, however, be reasonably foreseeable: in this case the behaviour of the manufacturer in contrast with legitimate safety expectations, in so far as related to uses that are 'reasonably foreseeable', is taken into consideration.

With respect to letter c), the reference of the evaluation of defectiveness at the time the product was put into circulation must be correlated with the provision of Article 118, which states that the responsibility of the manufacturer is excluded if the state of scientific and technical knowledge, at the time in which the manufacturer put the product into circulation, still did not allow the product to be considered defective. In other words, the product is not defective if the state of knowledge could not have made it possible for the product to be considered unreasonably risky at the time of its introduction on the market. The pertinent defect for the discipline under examination is, therefore, only the so-called original defect, or that which could be recognized at the time of putting the product into circulation. Defects which may be revealed thereafter and behaviours of the manufacturer to remedy, or at least reduce, the risk enter into a different realm of responsibility, founded on the general provisions and encompassed in the sphere of civil liability for negligence. The last paragraph of Article 117 sets out a further objective parameter, providing that a product is defective if it does not offer the safety normally offered by other items of the same lot. This deals with cases in which it is easier to identify the existence of a defect, since the term of comparison is given by the perfect regularity of the other items of the lot.

Finally, the rule provided in the second to last paragraph of Article 117 should be mentioned, according to which a product cannot be considered defective for the simple fact that an improved product has been, at any time, put on the market. To establish whether an expectation of safety is legitimate, the circumstance of prior, contemporary or subsequent circulation of an improved and, therefore, safer product has no bearing. The provision implicitly refers to defects in the manufacture and design: in relation to these types of defects, the fact that, with respect to the type of product taken into consideration, there is another, more advanced model on the market does not mean in itself that the level of safety of the first does not fulfil the 'reasonable expectations' of the public. The concept of 'state of the art' cannot in fact be adopted in an absolute sense. Different plans and methods fall within its ambit (both in design and manufacture), and some may be more advanced than others under a safety stand point, without such diversity, however, authorizing the formulation of tout court judgments on defectiveness. However, also for the application of the provision in question, the above-mentioned circumstances are important, in particular those set out in (a) and (b).

IV. Contracts with Users and Consumers

184. During the purchase of goods and the use of services, two different profiles can be distinguished: on the one hand, we must examine business activities, which in this phase regard the countless contracts through which the distribution of goods and services among consumers is carried out; while on the other hand, it is necessary to ascertain whether it is possible to offer protection to consumers who, in this case, assume the role of 'weak contracting parties', forced to accept the conditions imposed by enterprises without being able to negotiate or modify them.

185. While in matters of commercial advertising and defective products, the absolute lack of concern of the Civil Code for consumers is evident, on general conditions of contracts, the Code dedicates some provisions to consumer protection, leading other European systems in the legislative discipline of mass contracts. The law attributes effectiveness to general conditions of contracts: these are contractual conditions provided in a uniform way by one of the contracting parties (by the industrial manufacturer, the bank, the transport enterprise, etc.) and applicable to all contracts which are concluded with the consumers or users. In this regard, these contracts are known as standard contracts or mass contracts since their content is entirely predetermined by one of the two parties, while the other cannot negotiate, but only 'take it or leave it'. The rule provided by the Civil Code is that for which the general conditions of the contract are effective in regard to the other contracting party if, at the time of the conclusion of the contract, he/she has recognized them or should have recognized them through the use of ordinary diligence (Article 1341 paragraph 1). The actual knowledge of the contractual conditions is, therefore, substituted, as the needs connected with uniform contracting practice impose, by mere recognizability, so that the consumer or the user is bound by the contract even if he/she actually was unaware of its contents, and, therefore, could not have wanted it.

186. The second paragraph of Article 1341 provides some exceptions to the provision set out in the first paragraph in that so-called vexatious clauses must be specifically approved in writing (therefore, they must actually be understood and wanted, and not simply known). Vexatious clauses are the conditions which establish, in favour of those who set them, limitations of responsibility, the choice of terminating the contract or suspending its execution, deadlines in detriment to the weak party, limitations to the possibility of opposing exceptions, restrictions of the freedom to contract with third parties, tacit extension or renewal of the contract, arbitration clauses or derogations to the jurisdiction of the judicial authority.

187. For standard contracts, printed forms are often provided for, which, at the conclusion of the contract, are filled in with the name of the other contracting party and the terms of the contract not already printed on the form. Also here the Civil Code mitigates the sacrifice of the contractual freedom of the weak contracting party: clauses added in pen or typed on the form prevail over the printed ones, even when the latter were not crossed out (Article 1342).

In addition to the above provisions, we should also mention the provision that, though not expressly indicated by the Code, with respect to mass contracts, codifies the principle according to which, in situations of doubt, the clauses inserted in the general conditions of the contract or in the pre-printed forms provided by one of the contracting parties must be interpreted in favour of the other (weak) contracting party (Article 1370).

188. The above-mentioned provisions lead us to conclude that the law favours the contractual freedom of enterprises and provides few controls on standard contracts, other than formal ones. It is in fact sufficient to examine the above-mentioned provisions to see that the controls provided by the currently in force discipline are not adequate for the purposes of consumer protection: Article 1341 paragraph 1 places the burden of knowledge and recognizability of the general conditions of the contract on the consumer, thus aggravating his/her contractual position; the protection offered by Article 1341 paragraph 2 to the weak contracting party by excluding the effectiveness of the vexatious clauses which are not specifically approved in writing is merely theoretical since, if, on the one hand, a simple subscription is sufficient to make the contracting party aware of the responsibilities he/she is assuming, on the other hand, it guarantees the enterprise the possibility of introducing into the contract any type of clause that cannot be negotiated or amended by the adhering party; Article 1341 paragraph 2 can furthermore be interpreted as a provision authorizing the use of vexatious clauses, in the sense that, rather than preventing the enterprise from using them, it simply sets forth the way in which they must be used; with respect to Article 1370, we must note that its application is extremely scarce, since it is limited only to obscure clauses, and, therefore, the function of protecting the adhering party vanishes.

189. In addition to Articles 1341 (on unfair terms in contracts) and 1342 (on pre-formulated standard contracts), of the Civil Code, there is a specific discipline (Articles 33 et seq. and Article 142 of the Consumer Code) concerning the protection of consumers (the buyers of goods and services) against abuses of power by the seller or supplier and, in particular, against one-sided standard contracts and the unfair exclusion of essential contractual rights.

Law No. 52 of 6 February 1996, implementing EU Directive 93/13, introduced in the Italian Civil Code rules concerning the fairness of terms and conditions in 'contracts between professionals and consumers'. These rules, that were first inserted in the Civil Code (Articles 1469*bis*–1469*sexies*), have been substantially transferred in the Consumer Code in 2005.

Article 36 of the Consumer Code states that any clause containing unfair terms according to Articles 32 and 33, provided for in contracts stipulated between a 'professional' and a 'consumer', shall be deemed void and the contract shall continue to bind the parties upon the remaining terms, if it is capable of continuing in existence without the unfair terms. A professional is defined as any 'person or entity acting for purposes related to his/her trade, business or profession'. Any 'person acting for purposes which are outside of his/her trade, business or profession' is considered a consumer.

A contractual term which has not been individually negotiated shall be regarded as unfair if, contrary to the requirement of good faith, it causes a significant imbalance in the parties' rights and obligations arising under the contract, to the detriment of the consumer.

The terms and conditions providing for exclusions of a professional's liability, limitations or prerequisites for the consumer in adopting legal actions against the professional, consumer's implicit acceptance of terms not directly included in the contract, rights of first refusal are assumed as unfair. In general, the unfairness of a single contractual term shall be assessed by taking into account the nature of the goods or services for which the contract was concluded and by referring, at the time of conclusion, and all other circumstances attending the conclusion, of the contract. The compliance with the above-described provisions is easily enforceable not only by the single consumer but also by associations or entities carrying and representing their interests. Pursuant to Article 37, persons or organizations, having a legitimate interest under national law in protecting consumers may take action before courts or before competent administrative bodies for a decision as to whether contractual terms drawn up for general use are unfair, so that they can apply appropriated and effective means to prevent the continued use of such terms.

190. The picture should be completed then by mentioning the discipline of exemption clauses, which are very frequent in business contracts: they are agreements which transfer the contractual and extra-contractual risk from one party to the other, agreements on which the Civil Code provides several mechanisms of control. Article 1229 of the Civil Code, in fact, provides that any agreement which beforehand excludes or limits the liability of the debtor for malice or gross negligence is null and void, and any agreement releasing debtor from or limiting his/her liability in cases in which his/her behaviour or that of his/her assistants constitutes a violation of the obligations deriving from laws of public policy is also null and void.

These provisions also appear as guidelines in support of the enterprise, which is guaranteed a wide field of action, and immunity from any external control. In fact, the limits, although weak, of the control having been drawn (nullity of exemption clauses only in the exceptional event of malice or grave negligence), the law leaves parties great freedom to negotiate any exemption from or limitation to liability, without judging the contents and without taking into consideration the contractual disparity of the parties. With regard to the definition of public policy referred to in the second paragraph of Article 1229, it should be stressed that this definition is commonly given a restrictive interpretation, so that extra-contractual exemption clauses are usually held valid, even if directed at releasing the agent from the consequences of his/her own detrimental activity.

V. Sales and Commercial Practices

191. Through supervision of the methods of selling products and offering services it is possible to prevent unlawful practices and excessively burdensome or clearly unfair conditions which are used by enterprises for the sale of their products or services.

It should be noted that in addition to the traditional means of selling, which are expressed in sale contracts for products or services, or contracts for the supply of products or services, various other commercial practices relating to the distribution of products have for some time been in use. The definition of sales itself has evolved as a result of its necessary adaptation of civil provisions to consumer needs; this has led to the emanation of specific statutory provisions in some cases.

192. In the Italian system, instalment sales, mail order sales, extraordinary sales and liquidation sales have received explicit discipline. They are not always disciplined with a view to consumer protection: the discipline of instalment sales, for example, clearly favours the seller; that of extraordinary sales and liquidation sales, on the other hand, was crafted on the principle intended to guarantee free competition among sellers, and, therefore, appears to be directed at repressing unfair practices.

In particular, with regard to instalment sales, we have said that the relative discipline is intended to protect the seller more than the purchaser.

If it is, in fact, true that the phenomenon of instalment sales generally takes place in an economic situation in which the weakness of the contracting position of the purchasing party is evident, the discipline offered by the Civil Code (Articles 1523 et seq.) does not appear at all in line with the need for the protection of the purchaser. Instalment sales (provided by the Code in the form of conditional sales, a clause which can exist or be suppressed in instalment sale contracts) are based on three principles: (a) the seller is obliged to immediately consign the object to the purchaser, who acquires the right to its use; (b) the purchaser becomes owner of the object only at the time of payment of the last instalment; (c) the risks related to the object sold, and in particular the risk of destruction of the object, are transferred from the seller to the purchaser at the moment of consignment: therefore, if the object is destroyed before full payment of the price (i.e., while it is still the property of the seller) the purchaser must still continue to pay the price.

If at the agreed-upon deadlines for the payment of the individual instalments the purchaser does not pay the instalments of the price, the seller can obtain the termination of the contract; he/she cannot, however, obtain it for missed payment of a single instalment, or that is less than one-eighth of the total price. Once the contract is terminated, the seller requests the restitution of the object, but he/she must, in turn, return the already paid instalments (save for the right to keep a certain amount as compensation for the use that the purchaser has made of the object).

193. Legislative Decree No. 24/2002 introduced new provisions in the Italian Civil Code related to consumer protection in the sale of consumer goods. Pursuant to these new provisions (from Articles 1519*bis* to Articles 1519*nonies*) the seller must guarantee to the purchaser the full conformity of the good delivered to what was agreed during negotiations with the consumer. This discipline too has been transposed in the Consumer Code in 2005 (Articles 128–135).

According to the new discipline the seller is obligated to deliver the goods in conformity with the sale agreement, being otherwise liable to the consumer for a 'defect of conformity'. The law does not define the notion of 'defect of conformity'. However, there is a presumption of conformity when the good which has been delivered conforms to its standard use and to the description made by the seller or when it has the quality and guarantees that standard goods of the same kind have and it is appropriate for the particular use requested by the consumer.

The concept of a defect of conformity also includes the defect of manufacturing if the good is manufactured by the seller or under his/her or her responsibility. Such liability is excluded when, at the moment of the execution of the agreement, the consumer knew of said defect or he/she could not have knowledge of it through ordinary diligence.

The seller is liable to the consumer for any and all defects of conformity existing at the moment of the delivery of the good. The consumer is, therefore, entitled to the restoration of the conformity of the good, without expenses, by repairing or substituting it; the reduction of the price; termination of the agreement.

In any case, the seller's liability is limited to a term of two years from the delivery of the good. The consumer has to notify the seller the defect of conformity within a two-month term from the date in which the defect has been detected unless the seller has recognized or hidden its existence. Moreover, even if a third party in the chain of sale is responsible for the damage, the seller is liable to the consumer for a defect of conformity, but he/she may act for recovery within two years from the date of the performance of its indemnity obligation.

With regard to the guarantee, the law does not specify the subject obligated to grant the guarantee, but there is a general provision which points out that the consumer is protected by the rights provided in the Law and such rights are unprejudiced by the guarantee. The guarantee should also indicate its object, its duration, its territorial limits and the grantor's data and it should be in writing and in Italian.

The law provides that any agreement which is limiting or excluding the rights granted to the consumer is null and void.

VI. Indemnification for Damages Derived from Defective Products

194. One quality which is required from all industrial products, whatever their use may be, is the possibility of being used safely, without detriment to the physical integrity and possessions of the user. This concept of 'safety', present in the Italian Constitution in Article 41 paragraph 2, which imposes on the private economic initiatives the limit for the safeguard of 'human safety', assumed a precise legal and technical significance only with the enactment in Italy of Community Directive No. 374 of 25 July 1985 in matters of liability for damages due to defective products.

195. Before the enactment of the above-mentioned Directive, jurisprudence had recognized the right of consumers to be indemnified by enterprises on the basis of the general civil provisions which impose indemnification for any unjust damage caused by negligence (Articles 2043 et seq. of the Civil Code), as well as on the basis of the provisions concerning contractual liability for defects of the goods sold. Such provisions are not well adapted to the consumers' need for protection since they considerably limit the possibilities for consumers to be indemnified. On the basis of the general provisions regarding the subject of extra-contractual liability, consumers see their right to compensatory damages recognized only when they manage to prove the negligence of the damaged, while on the basis of the provisions regarding contractual liability for the defects of an object, consumers can hold liable only those who sold them the defective product.

If it is true that the enactment of the Community Directive brought the broadening of consumer protection, it should, however, be noted that recourse to the provisions referred to above still exists: in fact the new discipline provides a particular liability which arises on the basis of specific conditions established by it and that, rather than substituting it, is added to ordinary contractual and extra-contractual actions, that is, to the other types of provisions on liability which already protect the damaged party.

The same decree which gave application to the Directive (Presidential Decree No. 224 of 24 May 1988) expressly provides that 'the provisions of the present decree do not exclude or limit the rights which are attributed to the damaged party by other laws' (Article 15).

Also these rules have been moved to the Consumer Code (Articles 114–127).

196. After this noteworthy remark, let us examine what the new discipline provides.

Substantially reproducing Article 1 of the EEC Directive, Article 114 of the Code states that 'the manufacturer is liable for the damage caused by defects in his product'. Special attention must be given to the absolute nature of liability according to the new provisions, in contrast with the liability for negligence, which was judged as an inadequate solution to the problem. In reality, neither Article 1 of the Directive, nor Article 114 of the Code expressly state that the captioned liability ignores negligence. But, the fact that the new discipline has introduced such a liability on the part of the manufacturer can be easily inferred from the correlation of Articles 114 and 118. The former provision states that the manufacturer's liability is simply a consequence of a defect of his/her product, and does not call for requisites in addition to the existence of a defect. Article 118 specifically enumerates the cases of exclusion of liability, among which 'diligence' of the manufacturer does not enter. It follows that, once the existence of a defect in the product that has caused damage has been ascertained, it would be useless for the manufacturer to give proof that he/she used the required diligence in the design and manufacture of the product, since this releases him from liability only if he/she can prove one of the circumstances set forth in Article 118.

The parties entitled to compensatory damages are, first of all, those who have purchased a defective product from third parties or the manufacturer himself/herself. They are furthermore those entities who, though not owners of the defective product, used it on the basis of a specific contractual relationship (under lease, work relationship, etc.), or on the basis of a relationship of courtesy or a de facto relationship (relatives, friends). Finally they are those who, although not using the defective product, come to find themselves, accidentally or not, in its zone of risk, and are thus involved in the accident (bystanders).

197. After having given a definition of the product, Article 115 states that, pursuant to the law under examination, all manufactures of any movable good put into circulation are 'manufacturers', without distinction between finished products, component parts or raw materials. Those who present themselves to the public as manufacturers in that they affix, or have others affix, their own name, a mark or another distinctive sign to the product manufactured by others or to the product's package are considered equal to manufactures, and are, therefore, subject to the relative liability (Article 116). This is a substitutive liability; therefore, the damaged party still maintains the right to raise his/her claims against the actual manufacturer of the damaging product. Furthermore, when the manufacturer is not identified, the supplier who distributed the product in the exercise of a commercial activity is subject to the same liability if he/she fails to communicate to the damaged party, within three months of request, the identity and domicile of the manufacturer or of the person who supplied him with the products (Article 116).

198. With respect to the definition of defectiveness of the product (Article 117), we must refer to Chapter 4, §1, III.

199. On the basis of the examined provisions of the Code, the following can be indemnified: (a) damage caused by death or personal injuries; (b) the destruction or deterioration of an object other than the defective product, provided that it is of a type normally destined to private use or consumption and that it was mainly used by the damaged party for the above purposes (Article 123). A classification is, therefore, introduced of the cases which entitle the damaged party to compensatory damages vis-à-vis the potential broadness of the range of damages which can be indemnified: this is with the purpose of simplifying the a priori calculability of the risks of production and, therefore, allowing enterprises to plan the same through insurance or bank guarantees.

In this regard, it should be noted that civil liability for defective products and consumer protection represent two distinct problems, with ample overlapping areas, but also with vast, unrelated fields. If, in fact, the need for consumer protection has inspired a broadening of the total operative area of the instrument of indemnification for damage deriving from extra-contractual liability, the discipline of the liability of the manufacturer, therein examined, expresses the intention to operate a precise identification of the area of the damage which can be indemnified.

Moreover, also in this provision, the integrative character of the new discipline is confirmed, with the specification that the criteria indicated in the subject of indemnification have a bearing which is limited to the case provided in the law. As already evidenced, the new discipline is placed side by side with the remedies already provided in the Italian system in favour of those who suffer an unjust damage: for example, the absence in the new discipline of any reference to moral damages certainly does not imply that the damaged party should be refused the possibility of invoking the provisions set forth in Articles 2043 and 2059 of the Civil Code and Article 185 of the Penal Code.

The delimitation of the operative field of manufacturer's liability was not, however, realized through the selection of a fixed set of interests susceptible to indemnification, but through the enumeration of the events to which the damage from products can be connected. The law does not state that the new discipline is applicable exclusively in regard to injury to the interest of life, physical integrity and property, but rather that the provisions regulating indemnification can be invoked only when the fact originating the liability falls in the trilogy: death, personal injury, destruction of an object other than that of the defective product. The categorization, therefore, concerns the fact originating the indemnification and not the interest protected.

Finally, it is important to remember that exemption has been provided for damage to objects, with a view to limiting the controversies to those of only a certain economic importance: it has been fixed at the amount of EUR 387.00, thus making it possible only to have damages to objects having a value which exceeds that sum indemnified.

Italian product safety legislation is largely the result of the implementation of European Directives. Italy transposed the General Product Safety Directive (59/92/EEC) through Legislative Decree 115/95 of 17 March 1995, replicating the provisions of the Directive almost exactly. Article 5 of Decree No. 115/95 implementing the general product safety directive (59/92/EEC) lists the authorities responsible for ensuring that only safe products are placed on the market.

The competent authorities are the following: the Ministry for Economic Development, the Ministry of Health, the Ministry of Labour, the Ministry of the Interior, the Ministry of Economy and Finance and the Ministry of Transports. These authorities check, within their respective sphere of responsibility, that the products placed on the market are safe.

VII. The Role of Consumer Associations

200. The framework Law No. 281 of 30 July 1998 introduced significant reforms to the Italian system of consumer protection. It gives legal standing to consumer associations before the courts, to act in defence of consumers' collective interests. If an association proceeds with legal action on behalf of consumers, it also provides legal assistance during the law suit and may make a request for compensation as well. Moreover, such associations are given the opportunity of instituting conciliation proceedings through Chambers of Commerce, Industry, Craft and Agriculture (CCIAAs)

The Law of 1998 set up the National Consumers' Council (Consiglio nazionale dei consumatori ed utenti-CNCU) within the Ministry for Industry. The Council provides advice and recommendations on laws affecting consumers and on the implementation of Community policies; it encourages out-of-court settlement of disputes. The Law also set up a register of recognized national consumer associations at the Ministry.

VIII. Alternative Dispute Resolution and Consumers

201. Consumer-related disputes are increasingly dealt with through the use of alternative dispute resolution. The government has introduced measures to enhance the role of mediation and arbitration through the Chambers of Commerce.

Law 580 of 29 December 1993 'Reform of the Chambers of Commerce, Industry, Craft and Agriculture (CCIAA)' redefines the role of Chambers of Commerce and it grants; new to the system of chambers. This applies to the organization of services for alternative dispute resolution, formerly left to the discretion of a few Chambers, but now both a right and a duty for all Chambers of Commerce.

Chamber of Commerce mediation service aims at settling economic disputes, especially those arising between companies or companies and consumers. The mediator does not settle the dispute but he/she helps parties to find a mutually satisfactory settlement. Steps are being taken to promote conciliation procedures, to ensure it is provided by all chambers to a similar standard and to train conciliators to recognize national standards.

202. With Legislative Decree No. 130, adopted on 6 August 2015 and aimed at regulating the out-of-court procedures, both national and transnational, concerning consumers' protection, in the specific field of contract of sale or provision of services between professionals in Europe and consumers resident in Europe.

Such new discipline ensures to consumers the possibility to start claims before independent, impartial and transparent institutions; in this perspective, the Legislative Decree 130/2015 modified Article 141 of the Consumer Code, now stating that ADR bodies are the entities entitled to manage such procedures, and introduce, on this regard, Articles 141*bis*–141*decies*.

In any case, even if the consumer starts an out-of-court procedure, he will never be deprived of the possibility to apply to the Court.

IX. Class Action

203. In 2007, a regulation of collective redress was introduced in Italy through the Budget Law for 2008 (Law No. 244/2007). The Law provided for a collective action for the recovery of damages suffered by consumers. According to the Law, a consumers' association could bring a claim on behalf of a group of consumers who suffered damages from violations of specific rules by a company. The Law was amended in 2009, through Law No. 99 of 23 July 2009, which entered into force on 1 January 2010 and applied only to offences committed from 16 August 2009 onwards.

The Law introduced Article 140*bis* of the Consumer Code, which allows any single consumer or customer, on behalf of a class of consumers (an opt-in model has been chosen), to sue companies for damages arising from illegal behaviour. Illegal conducts which entitle to a class action are: the violation of contractual rights, including contracts stipulated according to Articles 1341 and 1342 of the Civil Code; the violation of rules on product liability; unfair commercial practices; antitrust infringements.

X. The Role of the National Competition Authority

204. With Legislative Decree 22/2014, adopted on 6 June, a new form of protection has been accorded to consumers: now, in fact, the National Competition Authority (AGCM) has been recognized with inquisitive and repressive powers, which are the same to which AGCM is entitled in the antitrust sector (*see* Part I, Chapter 3, paragraph 51 and Part II, Chapter 3, paragraph 167).

Chapter 5. The Italian Banking System

§1. Overview

205. The Italian banking system has been governed, for almost sixty years, by banking law of 1936.

With the law of 1936, an institutional despecialization of banking activity took place, in terms of time and technical form of the operations performed. In fact, there were banks that could only collect and use short-term funds (so-called credit companies) and other banks that could use them in the medium-long term (so-called credit institutes).

Furthermore, types of banks could have been even combined, because some of them were public-law entities (e.g., Banco di Napoli), while the others were set up as private companies. There was also a middle way represented by the banks of 'national interest', such as the Comit (Banca Commerciale Italiana).

At that time, banks were classified with a number of names (such as bank of national interest, ordinary credit companies, special credits institutions, etc.), and that affected even their operations, with the result that some of them were known as 'special credit' (e.g., land loan).

206. The situation has radically been changed with the Consolidated Law on Banking (Legislative Decree No. 385 of 1 September 1993), which is still in force.

Today, banks can easily carry out their business both in the short and in the medium to long term, thus overcoming the previous distinction between companies and credit institutions.

Other principles established by the TUB are:

- the bank shall be a company (subject to authorization for its establishment by the Bank of Italy);
- as such, the bank can only be set up in the form of a joint-stock company or limited liability company (legally public banks no longer exist);
- the bank which has its registered office in an EU country can freely establish itself in the Italian territory (i.e., the right to provide services freely throughout the EU applies, pursuant to the principle of mutual recognition).

As a result, those special credits that had a separate regulation and that now, on the other hand, maintaining certain rules of their own in certain cases, are absorbed within the normal banking activity.

207. Nowadays, banking activity can be performed through three different models:

(1) specialized banks (which is that existing before the Consolidated Law on Banking, and that now carries out certain specific operations);
(2) universal banks; and
(3) multipurpose banking group.

The universal bank is the bank that has no operational limits as regards both the duration of funding and loans (short, medium and long term), and the technical forms of operations it can perform.

A sound and prudent management is necessary to avoid the occurrence of the mingling of banks and companies that led in 1936 to the adoption of a banking law, precisely to avoid situations of crisis and illiquidity of the banks.

The multipurpose banking group is instead made up of a group of banks or other autonomous financial intermediaries, each with its own business, but all headed by a 'group leader'.

In other words, it is the case of a bank which, in order to carry out certain specific activities (e.g., credit in the form of factoring), constitutes other companies, i.e., other banking or financial entities legally distinct from it, while remaining the parent company of these new corporate organizations. A banking group is then created, linked by a common final design, in which each independent and autonomous subject is linked to the parent company by significant participatory or contractual ties.

§2. Banche Popolari and Cooperative Banks

208. The Italian Consolidated Law on Banking, has been recently modified by Law 33/2015, which affects the dispositions concerning 'banche popolari', which are a peculiar type of cooperative banks.

209. In particular 'banche popolari' are now those which did not overcome EUR 8,000,000,000.00 as total assets from the balance sheet; if the bank is the parent company, such threshold shall be considered from the consolidated financial statements.

The transformation in corporation shall be authorized by the Bank of Italy, which shall take into account the interest of creditors, along with the needs for patrimonial strengthening and system streamlining, along with compliance with the criteria of sound and prudent management. In case of transformation, shareholders may withdraw, as provided by Italian Civil Code and bank by-laws.

210. On 18 February 2016, Law Decree No. 18 was adopted to reform the cooperative banks (BCC) sector.

Cooperative credit is a national system that is divided into two directions: associative and entrepreneurial.

The association side is divided into three levels: local, regional and national. The Cooperative Credit Banks belong to the Local Federations (which have one or more regions and in total there are fifteen) which, in turn, are associated with Federcasse, the Italian Federation of BCC-CR, which performs functions of representation and protection of the category and legal, fiscal, organizational, communication, and training assistance for the entire Cooperative Credit System.

The Law Decree No. 18/2016 provides to reduce the fragmentation of the sector and to overcome the existing weaknesses deriving from the business model – clearly included in the trend of the environment of the reference territory – from the organizational structures and the size reduced by individual banks. The guidelines of the cooperative credit reform can be summarized as follows:

- confirmation of the role of the BCC as cooperative banks of communities and territories;
- better quality of governance and simplification of internal organization;
- a more efficient allocation of resources within the system;
- the timely retrieval of capital in the event of patrimonial tensions, also through the access of external capital to the cooperative world;
- the unity of the system to increase competitiveness and stability in the medium to long term.

§3. Banking Supervision

211. As a response of the 2008 financial crisis, the European Union pursued a number of initiatives that lead to the establishment of the so-called Banking Union, which is currently composed of two pillars, the Single Supervisory Mechanism (SSM) and the Single Resolution Mechanism (SRM). A third pillar, a European Deposit Insurance Scheme (EDIS), is currently under discussion.

In particular, with reference to supervision, the new enacted legislation provides that such task is conferred to European Central Bank (ECB), which undertakes the supervision activities in cooperation with national supervisors (National Competent Authorities - NCAs). Under the new rules, the most significant banks are subject to direct supervision of the ECB, whilst the less significant banks and financial institutions are subject to direct supervision of the NCAs and under indirect supervision of the ECB.

The distribution of responsibilities and tasks between the ECB and NCAs are set out in the SSM Regulation (Council Regulation (EU) No. 1024/2013 of 15 October 2013), which provides the relevant rules for the new structure of banking supervision and creates a new model of cooperation and interaction between EU and National administration, both at decision-making and at operational level.

The rules regarding SSM, which have come into effect on November 2014, apply to banks and financial located in the Euro area or located in countries that have joined the SSM.

Chapter 6. Other Provisions Affecting Entrepreneurial Activities

§1. Protection of the Environment in Civil Law

I. Preface

212. The development of the industrial society and the progressive impoverishment of natural resources have posed the problem of environmental protection. That problem touches various aspects, both legal and economic, but in Italy its principal point of reference has been the human being and the necessity of guaranteeing the conditions necessary for explication of the personality. Violations of the natural environment can in fact result in harmful effects on health and, in general, cause situations that can prevent the full development of human beings according to Article 3 of the Constitution. It is clear, therefore, that the health of humans can suffer damages from the degradation of the environment, and that the protection of the environment normally involves the protection of human health. However, if it is true that environmental degradation can cause damage to health, it is not also true that the damage to health always derives from damage to the environment or that the damage to the environment involves only objects and interests connected to health. The definition of environment has often exhausted itself in the bifocal polarization of the concepts of 'health' and of 'territory': the connection of those concepts is founded on the Constitutional text, where, on one side, the right to health is set forth as a fundamental right of the individual (Article 32), and, on the other, the protection of the landscape is expressly provided for (Article 9); this explains the purpose of merging the right to the environment and the right to health in the 'right to a healthy environment', an absolute right can be protected under civil provisions.

213. The current tendency, however, is directed at the configuration of an individual right in relation to the environment which is totally autonomous and separate both from the right to health and from the rights to property and other rights regarding the enjoyment of goods. Such right to the environment affirms itself as a right of personality and, as the right to health, it seems to fall among the fundamental inviolable rights of man guaranteed by Article 2 of the Constitution. This current trend is on target because it is certain that ecological problems have vast implications, all of which have to be faced through the actions of public powers, both under administrative and criminal profiles, and which can certainly not be resolved through mere specific and sporadic remedies of civilistic actions for protection offered by the system. In addition, after the Paris Agreement, adopted in 2015 under the United Nations Framework Convention on Climate Change (also known as COP21), such tendency has assumed an increasingly important role.

II. Prevention of Environmental Damage

214. Environmental politics are characterized by the emergence of strong conflicts: not only among antithetic interests for environmental protection, production and economic development, but also among collective interests which are all related to the protection of the environment (e.g., often the interest to create works to eliminate pollution conflicts with interests for environmental protection of the specific areas where the works are to be created).

In Italy also this has caused obstacles and delays in the accomplishment of organic environmental policies.

The Italian environmental legislation owes much of its inspiration to the Community legislation, of which it constitutes in the majority of cases a pure application: the majority of legal provisions issued in the course of the last decade make explicit reference to the EEC Directives on the subject of pollution, dangerous substances, information, prevention and protection of wildlife. Before the Community Commission was initiated, with the first programme of intervention, a uniform policy for the environment, Italy could count on a series of laws in this field, which rather than being expressly set forth for environmental protection and protection of human beings, were issued to defend nature like the law on maritime fishing (Law No. 963 of 14 July 1965), the law bringing provisions against atmospheric pollution (Law No. 615 of 10 May 1976 and its subsequent amendments), the law bringing provisions for the protection of the sea (Law No. 979 of 31 December 1982). In the footsteps of the two programmes of action of 1973 and 1977 of the European Community on the environment, three main steps have been taken: the definition of regional authority on protection of the environment from pollution (1977), the first general law on the disposal of waste (1982), the establishment of the Ministry of the Environment and the discipline on damage to the environment (1986), the organic law on the protection of the soil (1989), the first general plan for financial intervention for the environment (1990).

215. Although many of the provisions issued by the Italian Government over the course of the last two decades have been inspired by emergencies (e.g., drinkable water and seaside water, industrial waste and dangerous factories), the situation has evolved: from the discipline of individual areas or sub-areas of environmental policy there has been a move toward the definition of more general disciplines, which takes into consideration, all together, many profiles of environmental protection and the interactions among them.

In this regard the most significant innovations are the establishment of the Ministry of the Environment, the law on the evaluation of environmental impact and, finally, the adoption of the Environmental Code with Legislative Decree 3 April 2006, No. 152.

More recently, the European Commission adopted several acts in order to implement the objectives set forth by COP21.

216. With the institution of the Ministry of the Environment (Law No. 349 of 8 July 1986) a sphere of State intervention was identified for the protection of the environment and nature, which comprises and unifies policies for prevention of pollution and environmental clean-up, policies of planning and direct administration, and policies of direction and management. The goals of the Ministry are set out in Article 1 of the law which established it: ‘it is the duty of the Ministry to organically ensure the promotion, conservation and recovery of environmental conditions suiting the fundamental interests of the community and the quality of life, as well as the conservation and exploitation of the natural patrimony and the protection of natural resources from pollution.'

In addition to the Ministry, other entities (local autonomies and agencies) play a significant role with regard to environmental policies and protection. Regions, provinces and municipalities are entrusted with powers in different fields. Regions may legislate and have planning powers on waste management and disposal and water protection. Provinces and municipalities are also recognized planning powers. They all can grant environmental permits. Besides, the National Agency for Environmental Protection (ANPA) and the Regional Agencies for Environmental Protection (ARPA) have monitoring powers and can provide statements regarding compliance with environmental rules.

217. The same law of 1986 dictated provisions, on environmental damage and on environmental impact.

Environmental impact designates the action of a known physical cause on the environment. In this regard we can distinguish the current environmental impact, which is a set of effects produced from an existing work on surrounding territory, from the prediction of environmental impact, which, on the other hand, is the technical operation which analyses the environmental implications of a source of risk not yet existing, and tries to predict the negative environmental effects which presumably would be present if the work were carried out. The 'evaluation of the environmental effect' (VIA) is also spoken of, which is the operation with which, on the basis of special procedures, environmental compatibility is verified: that is, current or foreseeable impacts are quantified, attributing the same value judgments.

In light of the American, British and French experiences, as well as the EEC Directive of 27 June 1985, in Italy too the necessity of a verification of environmental compatibility for urban planning and new productive activities was called for by many. A decree of the President of the Republic of Italy (d.p.r. 12 April 1996) set out the main principles concerning the evaluation of the environmental effect (VIA) and it empowers the regions to implement the European directives and to lay down a detailed discipline on the issue.

The regulation of VIA was integrated with the adoption of the Environmental Code in 2006 (*see* current Chapter §1.IV).

218. Finally, the European Union nationally determined contribution (NDC) under the Paris Agreement is to reduce greenhouse gas emissions by at least 40% by 2030 compared to 1990, under its wider 2030 climate and energy framework. All key legislation for implementing this target has been adopted by the end of 2018.

III. Indemnification of Environmental Damage

219. The law which instituted the Ministry of the Environment also dictated specific provisions with regard to environmental damage. Article 18 of the law provided that malicious and negligent acts which damaged the environment obligated the infringer to pay compensatory damages to the State and to restore the places that were damaged to their prior state.

Thus, for the first time the interest of preservation of the environmental integrity was consecrated at an institutional level like an interest belonging to an individual. The action for the indemnification of environmental damage is, however, promoted by the State, in the person of the Ministry of the Environment, as well as by the territorial bodies to which the damaged assets belong. The citizens and associations for environmental protection can only report the damaging facts for the purpose of soliciting action on the part of the authorized bodies.

The law under examination provides a statutory discipline for public damage of pertinence to the State, damage transcending to the physical injury of assets composing the environment and comprising also the injury of other subjective situations belonging to local bodies, for instance, the detriment to the name and image of a Commune derived from instances of pollution.

The law also established clearer and more severe restoration, compensation and sanction profiles, since it provided for the obligation on the part of the judge to order in the conviction sentence, when possible, the restoration of the state of the places at the expense of the liable party, and the possibility of quantifying damages with equity, taking into consideration, however, the gravity of the negligence of wrongdoing, the cost necessary for restoration and the profit made by the transgressor as a consequence of his/her violation of environmental assets. It should be noted that the conviction for the restoration of the places assumes a dominant position among the forms of protection and constitutes the most appropriate remedy to adopt, since it is most suitable to suppress the source of future damage.

As well as the rules on VIA, the discipline of the environmental damage was modified and complemented with the adoption of the Environmental Code.

IV. The Environmental Code

220. The described legislation was consolidated in 2006 in a comprehensive piece of legislation – the Environmental Code – which was approved with the Legislative Decree No. 152 of 3 April 2006. The Code also updates the applicable rules and enacts the EC Directive No. 42/2001 in the field of Strategic Environmental Evaluation (VAS), the EC Directive No. 60/2000 on the defence of the soil and on water protection.

The Code regulates the evaluation of environmental impact, the management and disposal of waste, the protection of water, the defence of the soil, the reduction of the environmental pollution and the liability for environmental damage.

Following its entry into force, the Code was the object of different modifications and integrations. The Code was also complemented by many enacting regulations, which completed its scope of application.

V. The Environmental Crimes

221. The Environmental Code even introduced some environmental crimes, in addition to those contained in the Italian Criminal Code, and environmental crimes, such as the illicit waste smuggling, activities related to environment carried out in lack of authorization, and providing administrative and criminal fines.

222. Law 68/2015 added to the Italian Criminal Code a title introducing some new environmental crimes, such as environment pollution, environmental disaster (even due to negligence), smuggling and abandonment of highly radioactive waste, criminal association in environmental waste.

§2. Corporate Criminal Liability

223. The law on corporate criminal liability (Legislative Decree No. 231/2001) is implementing the OECD Convention on the corruption of foreign public officers in international transactions dated 17 December 1997.

The new rules have introduced a new type of liability on companies. The architecture of the new law is connected with the Federal Sentencing Guidelines (2000). The main aim of the new rules is to encourage companies to adopt codes of ethics and compliance programmes to prevent top managers, executives, employees and external collaborators from committing economic crimes against the State as well as other criminal offences.

Lack of compliance with internal codes triggers a type of company liability, which differs from previously existing civil and criminal liability, as it represents a sort of hybrid, mainly based on criminal liability.

Such liability applies to those 'corporate crimes which are committed in the interest (economic interest) or to the benefit of a company' by persons who are entrusted with the representation, administration or management of the company or by those persons who are subject to their authority or control. The company is not liable where the persons indicated above have acted in their own exclusive interest or in the interest of third parties.

Corporate liability remains autonomous from punishment reserved for the offender and applies to companies irrespective of the fact that the author of the crime has been identified or punished.

The corporate liability arises in respect of several crimes. The most important are the ones against the Public Administration (bribery and corruption, fraud, undue receipt of public facilities, computer crimes against the State or public bodies) and other corporate criminal offences such as false accounting, false corporate information in a prospectus destined to investors, false reports or communications by auditing companies, etc. Corporate liability is also provided for crimes connected to terrorism, slavery, pedopornography, money laundering, organized crime, intellectual property violations. Since 2007, this type of liability is also extended to crimes committed through the infringement of provisions on employees' safety.

224. Where criminal offences have been committed, the company can be subject to fines and sanctions of different nature (up to the prohibition for the company to carry on its activity on a temporary basis or to the prohibition to contract with the Public Administration). In addition, the company will, in all cases, be obligated to compensate third parties for damages.

To avoid liability the company must adopt and effectively implement a compliance programme capable of preventing crimes such as the ones committed. The law lays down the main elements of such compliance programmes. The internal rules shall:

- identify the sectors of its activity where it is most likely that crimes will take place;
- lay down measures to prevent such crimes;
- identify the safest way to manage financial resources as to avoid their commission;
- make it compulsory for all employees to supply the necessary information to the supervisory board entrusted with monitoring the operation of self-protection schemes and actual compliance therewith;
- provide for disciplinary measures necessary to ensure compliance with rules laid down in the schemes.

The law also empowers business associations to define standard guidelines for the adoption of compliance programmes by their member companies. Therefore, a compliance programme has to meet both the requirements fixed by the law and the guidelines laid down by the association in order to avoid any liability for the company.

In addition, it is now possible to certify the compliance by enterprises with the Legislative Decree No. 231/2001.

§3. Anti-Money Laundering

225. Legislative Decree 231/2007 adopted on 14 December, and its subsequent amendments and additions, introduced obligations concerning the prevention of money laundering and countering the financing of terrorism, imposing on banks and professionals, such as lawyers and accountants, to proceed to customer identification and the identification of the beneficial owner, that is:

- in case of a company: (i) the individual or individuals who ultimately owns or controls a legal entity through ownership or direct or indirect control over a sufficient percentage of the investments in the share capital or voting rights within that legal entity, or (ii) the individual or individuals who otherwise exercise control over the management of a legal entity;
- in case of other legal entities: (i) where the future beneficiaries have already been determined, the natural person or natural persons in receipt of 25% or more of the assets of a legal entity; (ii) where the individuals that benefit from the legal entity have not yet been determined, the class of persons in whose main interest

is established or acts as the legal entity, and (iii) the natural person or natural persons who exercise control over 25% or more of the assets of a legal entity.

By 10 January 2020, pursuant to Directive (EU) 2018/843, each Member State shall introduce an Ultimate Beneficial Owner (UBO) Register

§4. Data Protection

226. In 1996 Italy has enacted the EC Directive No. 95/46 on data protection through Law No. 675/1996. The initial period of application of the national rules on data protection has brought shortcomings and contradictions arising from rules which have no equivalent in the Community Directive. Notwithstanding the changes made over time, the rules on data protection still remained burdensome and costly to comply with.

The main aspects which are departing from the rules set out in the Directive are the following:

- consent to the processing of data. Article 7 of Directive 95/46/EC provides for much simpler rules than the Italian Law: consent must be given unambiguously, thus offering the individual the possibility of refusing consent, and hence applying the 'opt-out' procedure. The national rules of several Member States (United Kingdom, Germany, France, Spain) follow that principle. The Italian Law is much more burdensome on this point, as it has chosen an 'opt-in' procedure by requiring that consent must be 'freely expressed', 'specific' and 'documented in writing'. The national provisions, moreover, require consent to be given not only for processing data, but also for their communication;
- the protection of legal persons. The protection of legal persons falls within the scope of the national provisions notwithstanding the fact that the Directive is silent on this point. Therefore, Italy is one of the very few Member States which protects legal persons within the framework of data protection rules;
- the adoption of security measures. The national rules make a distinction between minimum and adequate security measures which are not contained in the European Directive. An entrepreneur who falls short in providing minimum security measures may face criminal sanctions.

227. In 2003, the Italian government has approved a code on data protection which replaced the existing laws and streamlined the procedures related to data protection. Italy's new Personal Data Protection Code (Legislative Decree No. 196 of 30 June 2003) has entered into force on 1 January 2004.

The Code consolidates all the legal provisions regulating personal data protection in Italy. Its principal purpose is to simplify and harmonize the existing legal framework. The Code strengthens the role of codes of conduct and professional practice. It is expressly set out that compliance with the provisions contained in codes of conduct shall be a general prerequisite for the processing of personal data by public and private entities to be lawful.

Simplification and effectiveness are the underlying principles with regard to exercise of data subjects' rights and the fulfilment of the relevant obligations by entrepreneurs.

The Code consists of three parts.

The first part sets out the general framework applying to all processing operations. In particular, section 1 explicitly declares that everyone has the right to the protection of personal data – a right which was recently reaffirmed also by Article 8 of the Charter of Fundamental Rights of the EU. Section 3 stresses the importance of the data minimization principle in reducing the amount of personal and identification data, with regard both to information systems and software.

The second part addresses the processing of personal data in specific sectors. Considerable attention is paid to processing operations by the police and in the judicial sector; as for processing operations carried out by public bodies for purposes of defence and/or relating to State security. It might also be pointed out that specific provisions address the processing of genetic data, biometric data and data disclosing geographic location of individuals, which are deemed to be more likely to affect data subjects' rights and freedoms. The Authority is granted power to further regulate these matters, by adopting detailed regulations.

Administrative and judicial remedies, sanctions, powers and functioning of the Authority are dealt by the third part of the Code.

228. Finally, on 14 April 2016, the EU Parliament approved the EU General Data Protection Regulation (GDPR), enforced on 25 May 2018 (Reg. 2016/679); it replaced the Data Protection Directive 95/46/EC and it is designed to harmonize data privacy laws of Member States and to protect and empower all European citizens' data privacy.

Article 4 GDPR introduced two figures in order to manage data acquired by a business:

- 'data controller', which is the natural or legal person, public authority, agency or other body which, alone or jointly with others determines the purposes of the processing of personal data;
- 'data processor', which is the natural or legal person, public authority, agency or other body which processes personal data on behalf of the controller;
- 'data protection office' (DPO), which is appointed by the data controller in order to monitor compliance with GDPR as regards the processing of personal data.

GDPR has a wide territorial scope: in fact, it applies to: (a) processing of personal data by controllers and processors in the EU or not and (b) processing of personal data of data subjects in the EU by a controller or a processor not established in the EU. In addition, non-EU businesses processing the data of EU citizens also have to appoint a representative in the EU.

Under GDPR, a number of rights is now recognized to data subjects; in particular:

- data subjects shall be informed in case of data breach;

- they shall obtain confirmation from the data controller as to whether or not personal data concerning them are being processed, where and for which purposes;
- data subjects shall be recognized the right to be forgotten (this right is also known as 'Data Erasure').

Selected Bibliography

AA. VV. *L'Antitrust Italiano.* Il Sole 24 Ore, Milano, 2003, a cura di Gustavo Ghidini.

AA. VV. *Codice commentato della Concorrenza e del Mercato.* Utet Giuridica, Torino, 2010, a cura di: Paolo Troiano, Antonio Catricalà.

AA. VV. *La Pubblicità Ingannevole*, Il Sole 24 Ore, Milano, 2003, a cura di Gustavo Ghidini.

AA.VV. *Trattato di diritto fallimentare.* Cedam, Padova, 2010, a cura di Vincenzo Buonocore, Amedeo Bassi.

AA.VV. *Il diritto dei consumatori.* Cedam, Padova, 2010, a cura di Giuseppe Cassano, Marco Eugenio Di Giandomenico.

AA.VV. *Commentario breve al diritto dei consumatori.* Cedam, Padova, 2010, a cura di Alessio Zaccaria, Giovanni De Cristofaro.

AA.VV. *Commentario breve al diritto delle società.* Cedam, Padova, 2011, a cura di Alberto Maffei Alberti.

AA.VV. *Il diritto dei consumatori.* Torino: Giappichelli, 2009.

AA.VV. *Il sistema amministrativo italiano.* Il Mulino, Bologna, 2009, a cura di Luisa Torchia.

AA.VV. *I nuovi contratti nella prassi civile e commerciale.* Torino: Utet Giuridica, 2008.

AA.VV. *La società 'pubblica' tra diritto privato e diritto amministrativo* (Atti del Convegno, Padova, 8 giugno 2007). Cedam, Padova, 2008, a cura di Vincenzo Domenichelli.

Abriani Nicolò, Cottino Gastone & Ricolfi Marco. *Trattato di Diritto Commerciale – Diritto Industriale.* Padova: Cedam, 2001.

Alpa Guido. *Introduzione al diritto dei consumatori.* Bari: Laterza, 2006.

Alpa Guido. *Corso di diritto contrattuale.* Padova: Cedam, 2006.

Bassi Amedeo & Buonocore Vincenzo (eds). *Trattato di diritto fallimentare.* Padua: Cedam, 2010.

Bemporad Simone & Reviglio Edoardo. *Le privatizzazioni in Italia – 1992–2000.* Roma: IRI, 2001.

Brandolini Elena. *Il contratto di agenzia nella normativa nazionale, internazionale e comunitaria.* Torino: Giappichelli, 2010.

Campobasso Gianfranco. *Diritto Commerciale.* Torino: UTET, 2008.

Capriglione Francesco. *Nuovo diritto societario ed intermediazione bancaria e finanziaria.* Padova: Cedam, 2003.

Selected Bibliography

Carlizzi Marco. 'La direzione e coordinamento delle società a partecipazione pubblica'. In *La governance delle società pubbliche nel d.lgs. n.175/2016* a cura di Guizzi Giuseppe. Milano: Giuffrè. 2017.

Carlizzi Marco. 'Etica e impresa bancaria: riflessioni critiche sull'art. 111-*bis* TUB', being published in *Riv. dir. comm.*

Cassese Sabino. *La nuova costituzione economica.* Bari:Laterza, 2004.

Catricalà Antonio & Troiano Paolo (eds). *Codice commentato della Concorrenza e del Mercato.* Turin: Utet Giuridica, 2010.

Cassano Giuseppe & Di Giandomenico Marco Eugenio (eds). *Il diritto dei consumatori.* Padua: Cedam, 2010.

Corapi Diego. 'La rappresentanza commerciale'. In *Trattato di diritto commerciale e di diritto pubblico dell'economia*, diretto da Francesco Galgano, III, Cedam, Padova, 1988, ristampa.

Costato Luigi & Pellizzer Franco. *Commentario breve al Codice dell'Ambiente (D. legisl. 3 aprile 2006, n. 152,).* Padova: Cedam, 2007.

De Cristofaro Giovanni & Zaccaria Alessio (eds). *Commentario breve al diritto dei consumatori.* Padua: Cedam, 2010.

De Nova Giorgio. *Il contratto di leasing.* 2a. edizione. Milano: Giuffrè, 1985. Di Cataldo Vincenzo. *I segni distintivi.* Milano: Giuffrè, 1993.

Di Sabato Franco. *Istituzioni di Diritto Commerciale.* Milano: Giuffrè, 2004.

Domenichelli Vincenzo (ed.). *La società 'pubblica' tra diritto privato e diritto amministrativo.* Padua: Cedam, 2008.

Dona Massimiliano. *Pubblicità, pratiche commerciali e contratti nel Codice del Consumo.* Torino: Utet Giuridica, 2008.

Enciclopedia Del Diritto. Milano: Giuffrè, 1958–2004.

Elli Gianmario & Zallone Raffaele. *Il Nuovo Codice della Privacy.* Torino: Giappichelli, 2004.

Falce Valeria & Gambino Alberto. *Lineamenti economico-giuridici dell'azione di classe.* Roma: Scuola di diritto, 2010.

Fauceglia Giuseppe. *Il franchising profili sistematici e contrattuali.* Milano: Giuffrè, 1989.

Fauceglia Giuseppe. 'I contratti bancari'. In *Trattato di diritto commerciale* (volume 3.2). Torino: Giappichelli, 2005.

Ferri Giuseppe. *Manuale di diritto commerciale.* Torino: UTET Giuridica, 2019.

Frignani Aldo. *Franchising. La nuova legge.* Torino: Giappichelli, 2004.

Fusi Maurizio & Testa Paolina. *L'autodisciplina pubblicitaria in Italia.* Milano: Giuffrè, 1983.

Gagliardi Andrea Filippo. *Pratiche commerciali* scorrette. Torino: Utet Giuridica, 2009.

Galgano Francesco. 'Il nuovo diritto societario'. In *Trattato di diritto commerciale e di diritto pubblico dell'economia* (diretto da), XXIX. Padova: Cedam, 2003. Galgano Francesco. *Storia del diritto commerciale.* Il Mulino. Bologna, 1976, 1a. edizione, 1980, 2a. edizione.

Galgano Francesco. *Diritto commerciale.* Bologna: Zanichelli, 2003.

Ghidini Gustavo. 'I limiti negoziali alla concorrenza'. In *Trattato di diritto commerciale e di diritto pubblico dell'economia*, diretto da Francesco Galgano, IV, Cedam, Padova, 1988, ristampa.

Ghidini Gustavo. *La concorrenza sleale.* Torino: Utet, 2001.

Ghidini Gustavo. *La riforma della legge marchi.* Padova: Cedam, 1995. Ghidini Gustavo (ed.). *La Pubblicità Ingannevole.* Il Sole 24 Ore, Milan, 2003. Ghidini Gustavo (ed.). *L'Antitrust Italiano*, Il Sole 24 Ore, Milan, 2003.

Ghidini Gustavo. *Profili Evolutivi del Diritto Industriale.* Milano: Giuffrè, 2008.

Giuri' Codice Autodisciplina Pubblicitaria 29 giugno 1988 n. 73. In L.C. Ubertazzi (a cura di), Giurisprudenza pubblicitaria. Vol. 3°. Milano, 1989, 105.

Guizzi Giuseppe. *Il mercato concorrenziale: problemi e conflitti.* Milano: Giuffrè. 2018.

Guizzi Giuseppe. 'La risoluzione nei rapporti con gli altri procedimenti e strumenti di soluzione delle crisi bancarie', in *Diritto della banca e del mercato finanziario.* 2018.

Lattanzi Giorgio. *Reati e responsabilità degli enti. Guida al D.lgs. 8 giugno 2001, n. 231.* Milano: Giuffré, 2005.

Libonati Bernardino. *L'impresa e le società.* Milano: Giuffrè, 2004.

Mandrioli Crisanto. *Corso di diritto processuale civile.* 3 volumi. Torino: Giappichelli Editore, 2003.

Manetti Michela. *Le autorità indipendenti.* Bari: Laterza, 2007.

Mangini Vittorio & Olivieri Gustavo. *Diritto Antitrust.* Torino: Giappichelli, 2000. Marasa', Masi, Olivieri, Spada, Spolidoro. *Commento sistematico della legge mar-chi.* Torino: Giappichelli, 1998.

Molinari Vincenzo, *L'attuazione del registro delle imprese.* Cap. V. Pellegrini Editore, 1996.

Novissimo Digesto Italiano, diretto da A. Azara ed E. Eula, Utet, Torino, 1957-1975, volumi 20, tomi 21, con appendici dal 1980 al 1987.

Pardolesi Roberto (a cura di). *Diritto alla riservatezza e circolazione dei dati personali.* Milano: Giuffrè, 2003.

Ricolfi Marco. *I segni distintivi. Diritto interno e Comunitario.* Torino: Giappichelli, 1999.

Roversi-Monaco Fabio Alberto. 'L'attività economica pubblica'. In *Trattato di diritto commerciale e di diritto pubblico dell'economia*, diretto da Francesco Galgano, I. Padova: Cedam, 1977.

Sena Giuseppe. 'I diritti sulle invenzioni e sui modelli industriali'. In *Trattato di diritto civile e commerciale*, già diretto da A. Cicu e F. Messineo, continuato da L. Mengoni, IX, 3. Milano: Giuffrè, 1976.

Torchia Luisa (ed.). *Il sistema amministrativo italiano.* Il Mulino, Bologna, 2009.

Ubertazzi Carlo. *Concorrenza sleale e pubblicità.* Milano: Cedam, 2008.

Vanzetti Adriano e Di Cataldo Vincenzo. *Manuale di Diritto Industriale.* Milano: Giuffrè, 2000.

Selected Bibliography

Index

The numbers here refer to paragraph numbers.

Index

www.ingramcontent.com/pod-product-compliance
Lightning Source LLC
Chambersburg PA
CBHW071349230926
51846CB00002B/487
9789403534251